Essential Equine Studies

BOOK TWO

HEALTH, NUTRITION & FITNESS

JULIE BREGA

J. A. Allen
LONDON

ACKNOWLEDGEMENTS

Thanks to:

Nancy Clarke MSc who provided the original text on equne behaviour for Chapters 1 and 2.

Dr Catherine Dunnett BSc PhD R.Nutr for her advice and invaluable contribution to Chapters 3, 4, 5, and 6.

© *Julie Brega, 2005*
First published in Great Britain 2005
Reprinted 2009

ISBN 978 0 85131 909 4

J.A. Allen
Clerkenwell House
Clerkenwell Green
London EC1R 0HT

J.A. Allen is an imprint of Robert Hale Limited

www.halebooks.com

A catalogue record for this book is available from the British Library

Design by Judy Linard
Edited by Martin Diggle
Colour separation by Tenon & Polert Colour Scanning Limited, Hong Kong
Printed by Kyodo Nation Printing Services Co., Ltd, Thailand

BOOK TWO
HEALTH, NUTRITION & FITNESS

CONTENTS

LIST OF FIGURES

LIST OF TABLES

CHAPTER 1

HEALTH IN THE HORSE

The aims and objectives of this chapter are to explain:

- How a healthy horse will appear physically.
- The physical signs of ill health.
- When to call the vet.
- The horse's psychological needs.
- How horses interact with each other within the herd.
- The signs of psychological problems.

SIGNS OF GOOD HEALTH

Good management will increase the likelihood of horses in your care remaining healthy and sound. Early recognition of ill health will improve the horse's chances of a quick and complete recovery. Good health is indicated by a number of factors, the most significant being the following.

GENERALLY OBSERVED SIGNS

Alert outlook. When fit and well, most horses are alert, showing interest in their surroundings. They react to a variety of stimuli, such as feeding time, other horses passing by, loud noises, etc. and generally have an interested yet relaxed attitude.

Appetite. Most horses have a healthy appetite and clear up their feeds immediately. However, others are slow feeders, inclined to be a bit fussy about what they eat. If this is normal for a particular horse then don't worry if he is slow to eat up. Experimentation may be necessary to determine the ideal food for the fussy eater. However, if a usually enthusiastic eater doesn't finish his feed it is likely to be a sign that something is wrong.

Clear eyes and clean nostrils. The eyes must be bright and, like the nostrils, free of discharge, particularly that of a thick, sticky consistency. Occasionally horses have a slight clear, watery discharge – if no other symptoms are present, this can be considered as normal.

Skin and coat. The skin should feel supple and relatively loose. As you run your hand over the skin you should see small 'ripples' appear. The coat should have a smooth and naturally glossy appearance.

Normal excretion. The droppings should be passed regularly and will vary in colour and consistency according to the diet. A stabled horse eating mainly hay and short feed will pass yellow-brown droppings. The droppings should be fairly firm, breaking apart on hitting the ground, and should be free of any offensive odour. The droppings of a grass-kept horse will be of a softer consistency and dark green-brown in colour.

Micturition or urination (**staling**). Horses urinate approximately four to six times per day, passing between 5–15 litres (1–3.3 gallons) depending upon water intake and diet. Most horses wait until they are standing over bedding or grass before staling as they don't like to do so on concrete, or in a lorry without straw or shavings down. In such situations, they'll often wait until they return to their stable or field.

Horses adopt a typical posture when staling – they stand with their hind legs separated, leaning forwards slightly. Geldings normally extend their forelegs forwards as well. The horse may grunt as he stales.

The urine should be pale yellow to amber in colour and free of any offensive smell.

The limbs. The limbs should be free from heat, pain and swelling. The horse may stand resting a hind leg, but never a foreleg. He should be happy to stand bearing weight on all four limbs. When moving he must be sound, taking even, free steps. The walls of the hooves should feel uniformly cool, should free from excessive cracks and should be well trimmed / shod. The clefts of the frog should be free of offensive odour and discharge.

MEASURABLE SIGNS
The Mucous Membranes

A simple check of the mucous membranes can be carried out as part of a general observation of the horse's health, but it can also be used as a more serious check if conditions such as dehydration or shock are suspected. The gums of a healthy horse should be moist, slippery to the touch and salmon pink in colour. The **capillary refill** time can be checked by pressing the thumb on an area of the mucous membrane above the teeth to 'blanch' the area. Release the pressure and count how many seconds elapse before the colour (blood) returns to the area. The normal time taken is 1.5 seconds. Delays of 2–3 seconds are cause for concern – this indicates that the horse is slightly dehydrated. Delays of over 4 seconds are serious and are an indication of reduced blood circulation resulting from blood loss or dehydration and / or decreased blood pressure (shock).

Condition

Again, the horse's overall condition can be briefly assessed by an experienced person as a brief overview, along the following lines. Whatever his actual level of fitness, he horse should give an overall impression of well-being and should have an adequate good covering of flesh, preferably without being significantly overweight. However, condition can be evaluated more precisely by a process called **condition scoring**, in which a horse's condition can be assessed using the following scoring criteria.

Condition score 0 – very poor: rump sunken, the skin tight over prominent bones, spine and pelvis very prominent, marked ewe neck, very narrow.

Condition score 1 – poor: rump sunken, ribs prominent, spine and croup prominent, ewe neck, narrow and slack.

Condition score 2 – thin: rump flat either side of spine, ribs visible, narrow but firm neck.

Condition score 3 – good: rump rounded, ribs covered but easy to feel, neck firm, no crest.

Condition score 4 – fat: rump too rounded, gutter along the spine, ribs and pelvis difficult to feel.

Condition score 5 – obese: bulging rump with deep gutter along spine, ribs cannot be felt, crest, folds and pads of fat.

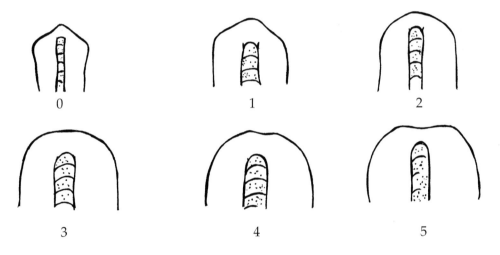

Figure 1 Condition scoring

A more detailed method of condition scoring can be used by applying the standard US body condition scoring system. With this system (see Table 1), each area of the body is assessed individually, the scores being totalled, then averaged to give the overall condition score.

Hint: when using this system, score the neck first visually and then feel for fat: repeat for withers, loin, tail head (i.e. top of tail), ribs and finally shoulder. Add scores and then divide by six to give the condition score.

> ITQ 1 What is meant by 'condition scoring'?

Condition score	General condition	Neck	Withers	Loin	Tail head	Ribs	Shoulder
1	Very poor	Individual bone structure visible	Bones easily visible, no fat	Spine bones visible; ends feel pointed	Tail head and hip bones very visible	Ribs very visible and skin furrows between ribs	Bone structure very visible
		Animal extremely emaciated: no fatty tissue can be felt					
2	Very thin	Bones just visible; animal emaciated	Withers obvious, minimal fat covering	Slight fat covering over vertical and flat spine projections; ends feel rounded	Tail head, hip bones obvious	Ribs prominent and slight depression between ribs	Bone structure can be outlined
3	Thin	Thin, flat muscle covering	Withers accentuated with some fat cover	Fat build up halfway on vertical spines but easily discernible; flat spinal bones not felt	Tail head prominent; hip bones appear rounded, but visible; pin bones covered	Slight fat cover over ribs; rib outline obvious	Shoulder accentuated, some fat
4	Moderately thin	Neck some fat, not obviously thin	Withers not obviously thin, smooth edges	Slight ridge along back	Fat can be felt	Faint outline visible	Shoulder not obviously thin
5	Moderate	Neck blends smoothly into body	Withers rounded over top	Back level	Fat around tail head beginning to feel spongy	Ribs cannot be seen but can easily be felt	Shoulder blends smoothly into body
6	Moderately fleshy	Fat can be felt	Fat can be felt	May have slight inward crease	Fat around tail head feels soft	Fat over ribs feels spongy	Fat layer can be felt
7	Fleshy	Visible fat deposits along neck	Fat covering; withers are firm	May have slight inward crease down back	Fat around tail head is soft and rounded off	Individual ribs can still be felt	Fat build-up behind shoulder
8	Fat	Noticeable thickening of neck	Area along withers filled with fat	Crease down back evident	Tail head very soft and flabby	Difficult to feel ribs	Area behind shoulder filled in flush with body
		Fat deposited along inner buttocks					
9	Extremely fat	Bulging fat	Bulging fat	Obvious deep crease down back	Building fat around tail head	Patchy fat over ribs	Bulging fat
		Fat deposits along inner buttocks may rub together; flanks filled in flush					
Score							

Table 1 Standard US body condition scoring system for horses

ITQ 2 On the 1-5 scale, how would a horse with a condition score of '3' appear?

ITQ 3 Describe how the mucous membranes of the gums should appear in a healthy horse.

Temperature, Pulse and Respiration (TPR)

Although commonly written as TPR (temperature, pulse and respiration), when recording these rates it is better to monitor the respiratory rate first. This can be done without stimulating the horse, which would cause an increased, and therefore inaccurate, heart rate. Next, take the pulse rate while the horse is still relaxed. Leave taking the temperature until last, since inserting a thermometer into the horse's rectum can upset a nervous type and, unless the horse is very used to the procedure, it will nearly always cause an increase in the horse's heart and respiratory rates.

To gauge what is normal for each individual horse, take the TPR first thing each morning for several days and write down the readings. The normal rates for a healthy adult horse at rest are as follows:

Temperature 100.4 °F (38 °C).
Pulse 25–42 beats per minute.
Respiration 8–16 breaths per minute.

To Observe Respiration

1. The horse must be standing still, at rest.
2. Watch the rise and fall of the flanks. Each complete rise and fall is one breath.
3. Count either the rise or fall for one minute.

The normal rate of respiration for an adult horse at rest is between 8–16 breaths per minute and, in the healthy horse at rest, his breathing should be hardly noticeable. The rate is higher in youngstock. As well as the respiratory rate, note the pattern and nature of the breathing. Is it laboured or irregular?

To Take the Pulse (Heart) Rate

The pulse rate can be taken by lightly but positively pressing the index and middle finger on one of the following arteries:

1. **Transverse facial artery** – level with and slightly behind the eye.
2. **Sub-mandibular artery** – inside edge of the lower jawbone.
3. **Palmar digital arteries** – level with the proximal sesamoid bones and at the rear of the pastern.
4. **Coccygeal arteries** – midline of the underside of the tail.

A stethoscope can also be used. This should be pressed against the horse's girth just behind the left elbow. Each 'lubb-dub' sound heard represents one heartbeat.

Whichever method you use, in order to count the pulse rate/heartbeat accurately, count for 1 minute. While the pulse rate of an adult horse at rest is between 25–42 beats per minute, foals will have a pulse rate of 50–100 beats per minute. The character of the pulse is also important, see **Increased pulse rate** in Signs of Ill Health.

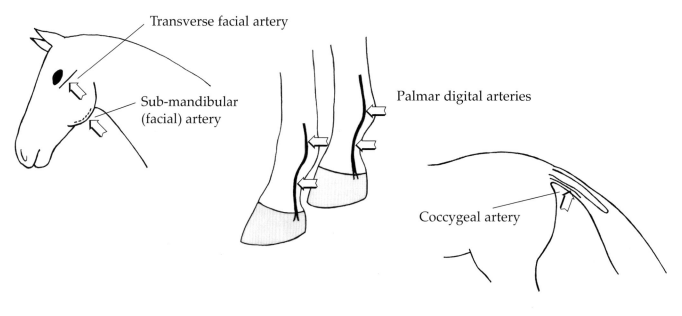

Figure 2 Sites for taking the pulse

To Take the Temperature

The horse's temperature is usually taken per rectum.

1. If the horse is unknown to you he should be untied and held. This is to prevent him pulling back and breaking the weak link should he become upset by the procedure.

2. If using a mercury thermometer, shake it down so that it reads several degrees lower than normal. It takes practice to read the mercury thermometer – digital thermometers are easier to read and safer to use. Switch on the digital thermometer and lubricate the end with petroleum jelly or saliva. Stand behind the horse, slightly to one side.

3. Hold the horse's tail to one side and insert the bulb of the thermometer approximately 5 cm (2 in) and hold at a slight angle to press the thermometer against the side of the rectum to avoid faecal matter.

4. Hold in position for one minute or, if using a digital thermometer, until the digits stop flashing or the thermometer 'beeps' to indicate that it has reached the maximum reading.

5. Withdraw and read the thermometer. Always wipe it clean and disinfect before returning to its case. Disinfectant wipes or surgical spirit and cotton wool are a convenient way of doing this.

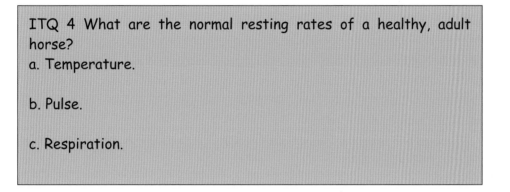

ITQ 4 What are the normal resting rates of a healthy, adult horse?
a. Temperature.

b. Pulse.

c. Respiration.

You will develop an eye for health and condition through constant observation. The most important consideration is to be aware of what is normal for each particular horse. Regularly check the limbs, TPR, etc., so you are familiar with the norm – this way any deviation will be more easily recognized.

SIGNS OF ILL HEALTH

We now discuss the signs of ill health. A horse may show only one or two of the following signs – it is up to you to notice the sign/s in the first instance and then to act accordingly. If you do notice any of the following signs you should:

● Look for additional signs which will further indicate the nature of the problem.
● Use this additional information to assess the problem.
● Decide whether or not to call the vet.
● Prevent the condition from worsening whilst waiting for the vet.
● If you decide the vet is not needed:
  – identify the cause
  – treat the problem
  – take steps to prevent it from occurring again.

Disinterested, dull attitude. Unless the horse is dozing, standing in the corner of the stable or field with the head low could be an early sign indicating that all is not right. If at grass, the horse may be standing further away from his group than usual.

Loss of appetite. If the horse fails to clear up a feed and is not interested in his hay or water, you should be on the lookout for further signs. However, bear in mind that a new horse in a yard may take a day or two to settle in and start eating properly.

Difficulty in eating. If the horse drops food from his mouth (known as **quidding**) it may indicate sharp edges or other problems with the teeth.

Dull and staring coat. This could be caused through being cold, through worm infestation, nutritional deficiency or a general lack of condition.

Tight skin. Dehydration causes the skin to lose its elasticity and feel 'tight'. The **skin pinch test** is used to check for this – take a fold of skin on the point of the horse's shoulder or neck between the thumb and forefinger, lift it away from the underlying tissue, twist slightly and release. When you let go of the skin it should return immediately to its normal position. If a skin fold or 'tent' remains for 2 seconds, the horse is mildly dehydrated. A delay of 5 seconds indicates serious dehydration.

Another test for dehydration, the capillary refill test, was described earlier (Signs of Good Health).

Sweating. Rule out the obvious first – the horse may be too warm, e.g. if wearing excessive rugs in mild weather, after strenuous exercise, etc. However, if there is no obvious reason, this could be caused by excitement or pain. Therefore, having ruled out obvious reasons, look out for other signs, especially those of colic.

Signs of colic. The horse may show one or more of the following in any combination:
- patchy sweating
- pawing at the ground
- looking round at the flanks
- kicking at the belly
- attempting to lie down, giving the appearance of 'crumpling', then getting up again
- repeatedly lying down and getting up
- rolling
- lying flat out in the stable
- increased pulse and respiratory rates
- loss of appetite
- dull attitude.

ITQ 5 What is the 'skin pinch test' and why is it used?

Lack of condition. This is fairly easy to recognize. A horse in poor condition usually has a dull coat, does not carry enough flesh, and may have projecting hips, shoulders and ribs if he is very thin. Using the condition scoring system mentioned earlier, a score of '2' is thin, '1', poor and '0', very poor. Horses don't normally lose condition overnight so poor condition is indicative of an ongoing problem which needs to be dealt with.

Rapid weight loss for no apparent reason can be indicative of a serious problem and the vet should be consulted.

Abnormal discharges. When emanating from the eyes and nostrils indicates either an infection such as a cold or influenza, especially if accompanied by coughing. If the horse is allergic to the dust found in hay and straw he may have a thick yellow (mucopus) nasal discharge accompanied by a cough.

Discharge from the eye only, especially if the lids and/or membranes are inflamed, may indicate a foreign body or condition such as conjunctivitis.

Abnormal mucous membranes. If the membranes of the eye and gums are abnormal in colour/texture, this may indicate certain conditions as follows:
- pale coloured – anaemia
- yellow (jaundiced) – liver problem
- deep red and dry – fever
- red with blue/purple tinge – pneumonia
- tacky and dry – dehydration.

Abnormal droppings. Again, certain abnormalities may suggest certain conditions:
- too hard – constipation
- no droppings – constipation or impaction (blockage)
- too soft/loose – worm infestation, excitement, too much rich grass, sharp teeth preventing efficient mastication, change in diet
- diarrhoea – infection such as salmonella, or poisoning.

Abnormal urine/urination. As with the mucous membranes and droppings, certain abnormalities may point to specific conditions:
- thick and cloudy and/or bloodstained – kidney disease
- smelling of violets and dark coloured – exertional rhabdomyolysis (azoturia)
- repeated efforts to urinate without producing any urine – kidney problems, cystitis.

Limb abnormalities. These may be broadly categorized as follows:
- Cold swellings, also referred to as 'filled legs', often arise from poor circulation caused by lack of exercise. They may affect older horses whose joints have been subjected to 'wear and tear'. Cold swellings are frequently not accompanied by lameness. Once the horse has been turned out or exercised the swelling often recedes.

- Hot swellings may be caused by impaired circulation, infection or injury, e.g. sprain, joint infection. The swelling may or may not be painful, and the horse may be lame. Hot swellings around joints need urgent veterinary attention as this may indicate an infected joint capsule which can be life-threatening. Investigation will be necessary to establish the cause of the swelling.

- Heat in one or more hooves may indicate a problem such as infection (pus in the foot) or laminitis.

- It is normal for a horse to rest a hind leg, but never a foreleg. A pottery, stilted action is indicative of **laminitis**. The laminitic horse will also stand with the weight back on his heels and will be reluctant to move. He may shift his weight from one front foot to the other.

Lameness. Lameness is a disturbance of the horse's natural gait, normally caused by pain or associated with the presence or aftermath of an injury that affects correct limb function. Thus it is a sign that disease or injury is, or has been, present. Examination of the horse is necessary to find out which leg is affected and the nature of the disease or injury.

It is necessary to be able to differentiate between lameness, as caused by disease or injury and a defective gait, as caused by faulty conformation or stiffness, arising from age or fatigue.

Fever. A rise in temperature of one or two degrees indicates pain, e.g. colic or injury. A rise of more than two degrees indicates a more serious infection.

Increased pulse rate. A rapid pulse of 43–50 beats per minute indicates pain, above that indicates fever. A very weak pulse indicates that the heart is failing, e.g. when a horse is in shock.

Increased respiratory rate. An increased rate may indicate pain. Laboured breathing and respiratory distress indicates damage to the lungs, e.g. recurrent airway obstruction (formerly called chronic obstructive pulmonary disease, or COPD).

Wounds. Any break in the skin or contusion (i.e. a wound) needs to be assessed and treated. Simple wounds can be cleaned and, if necessary, protected. Check that the horse is vaccinated against tetanus. More complicated wounds may need to be stitched or stapled, requiring veterinary attention. The heel region should be checked for cracking and mud fever in wet conditions, particularly if the horse is turned out in a muddy paddock.

ITQ 6 List five signs of colic.

ITQ 7 How should the urine of a healthy horse appear?

ITQ 8

a. What disease causes the horse to move with a pottery, stilted action?

b. What other signs accompany this disease?

WHEN TO CALL THE VET

Keep the vet's telephone number displayed near every phone to minimize delay, and make sure that it is entered into the mobile phones of all yard personnel. Consult the vet for any of the following situations.

Suspected colic. Call the vet out if the horse shows even very mild signs of colic for twenty minutes or more, or immediately if the horse shows violent colic signs. The vet will give analgesic (pain-killing) and muscle relaxant injections as even a mild case of colic can soon worsen; a horse in great pain will roll and thrash about, risking further injury and life-threatening complications such as a twisted gut, which requires surgery. If the horse needs surgery, the earlier he gets into theatre, the greater his chances of recovery.

Wounds. If a wound:
- is very deep or complicated
- is on a joint
- requires stitching
- is bleeding profusely
- is spurting blood (indicating arterial bleeding)
- has punctured the sole of the foot.

The vet will also be needed if there is any doubt about status of the horse's tetanus immunity. A quick-acting tetanus anti-toxin will be needed.

Lameness. If a horse is lame and you cannot determine the reason. If a horse is not bearing weight on a limb the vet must be called immediately.

Suspected fracture. Any suspected fracture, however caused, requires immediate veterinary attention. Injuries of this nature do not occur only in strong work or competition; accidents can happen while the horse is being hacked quietly, or even when turned out to grass.

Repeated coughing. The horse may or may not have a purulent discharge from one or both nostrils.

Abnormal temperature. A variation from normal of more than 1 °F.

Difficulties in foaling (dystocia).

Other than this, a general guide is to call the vet when your horse is showing any of the signs of ill health described earlier and you are unable to determine why, or to administer the necessary treatments. In particular, watch for loss of appetite and a dull attitude. These could be early warning signs of infection.

The horse should not be worked if he is showing signs of ill health. Apart from being unfair on him, and risking aggravating the condition, a sick or lame horse is unlikely to perform well enough to make any form of work constructive.

Veterinary Visits

Whenever the vet is to visit your yard, try to ensure that the following measures are taken.

- If possible, the horse is in a dry, well-lit loose box.

- Warm water, soap and towel are available for the vet to wash hands before and after treatment.

- If it could be relevant, any droppings that the horse has passed recently are kept in a skip. This may be helpful to the vet.

- A record is kept of all relevant information, including any food the horse has eaten and when, as well as any other signs of abnormalities.

ITQ 9 In terms of a suspected colic, when would you call the vet?

ITQ 10 In terms of wounds, when would you call the vet?

THE HORSE'S PSYCHOLOGICAL NEEDS

In addition to being able to recognize when a horse is in good or poor physical health, it is essential to appreciate his psychological needs in order that the best environment can be provided.

Many of today's domesticated horses live in relative isolation, spending large amounts of time stabled and, when turned out, they tend to be in small groups in relatively small paddocks.

Understanding how horses would behave in the wild, i.e. if feral, helps when planning a management regime, and this section looks substantially at feral behaviour. Some examples of the different types of areas where feral herds have been observed and exist today include the Carmargue in Southern France, mountainous and desert regions of North America (Montana and Nevada), outback regions of Australia (where the feral horses are referred to as 'Brumbys'), Przewalski horses in the Mongolian Steppes and various types of native pony dispersed throughout the British Isles (including New Forest, Dartmoor and Exmoor ponies).

While some of the activities discussed (e.g. feeding) may appear to be primarily physical, it is important to understand the instincts associated with them if (in the example of feeding) ailments such as colic (which can be stress-related) or injuries arising from bullying are to be avoided. Although the same conditions may not always pertain, or be viable, in domesticated circumstances as in the wild, existing facilities and regimes can often be adapted to take account of natural behaviour.

SEXUAL BEHAVIOUR

The sexual and reproductive behaviour of horses forms a very important part of the herd's social interaction and is correspondingly complex. The gender of the horse directly determines and influences the reproductive behavioural tendencies that the horse will exhibit. The horse's gender is determined genetically and during the embryonic stage **gonads** will develop. The female gonads develop as ovaries, the male gonads develop as testes. The gonads release reproductive hormones (**oestrogens** and **androgens**) during foetal development and after birth, from puberty onwards. These hormones stimulate sexual behaviour; however, the sexual and reproductive behaviour of each herd member will differ according to the individual horse's age, learning and previous experience, the surrounding environmental conditions and individual differences in personality.

The Sexual Behaviour of the Mare

In the northern hemisphere the breeding season normally begins around February/March and ends around September/October, with the oestrus cycle occurring regularly throughout this time; all mares will vary individually.

The majority of mares are sexually mature at around two years of age, although some early foals may ovulate as yearlings (and some Thoroughbreds do not mature until around four years of age). During the period between October and February there is no ovarian activity – this is known as **anoestrus**. A mare comes into season as a result of hormonal changes.

There are three natural factors in early spring that instigate the first of the hormonal changes:

- the rise in temperature
- extended daylight hours
- the improvement in the quality of the grass.

(In some breeding industries, e.g. Thoroughbred breeding, these factors are artificially induced through the use of heat lamps and lights in the stables and an increased nutritional plane via concentrates, in order to get the mare's cycle starting as early as possible. Hormone treatment is also frequently used. This is because Thoroughbreds all have their 'official birthday' on 1st January and thus it is desirable for Thoroughbred foals to be born as early as possible in the year.)

The usual length of the whole oestrus cycle, that is the period between the first day of heat in one cycle and the first day of heat in the next, is generally between 20 and 22 days. This, again, can vary from month to month and from mare to mare. Dioestrus, sometimes referred to as interoestrus, is the period between the last day of one heat and the first day of the next; this is usually 14–16 days. The mare's interest in, attraction to and acceptance of the stallion are largely determined by her sexual cycle. During the anoestrus and dioestrus phases, the mare fails to display any sexual interest in the stallion. Indeed, it is not unusual for a dioestrus mare to respond to a stallion with aggressive behaviour such as squealing, biting and kicking with the hind or front legs.

During oestrus, however, the mare's attitude to the stallion changes. It is common for both the mare and stallion to show interest in each other and correspondingly make a significant effort to actively seek each other out: the mare may sometimes disrupt any interactions between the stallion and other lower ranking mares. Most notably, the mare will tolerate the stallion's more frequent and persistent invasions of her personal space, which may result in mutual grooming. The mare may also adopt a braced posture to attract his attention (also referred to as the 'saw horse stance'). This involves the mare lowering her neck and hindquarters, contracting her abdomen and exaggerating the spacing between her hind legs. Frequent but small amounts of urine are passed and this is accompanied by the tail being held to the side in order to regulate 'winking' of the vulva and clitoris. This behaviour provides the stallion with a visual display of the mare's reproductive behaviour, and is also thought to help circulate the mare's pheromones and therefore attract the stallion's attention. If the mare is sexually receptive she will welcome the stallion's mounting behaviour by maintaining the braced posture and encouraging copulation (Although the basic features of the mare's sexual behaviour have been detailed here, it is important to remember that individual differences are demonstrated.)

ITQ 11 When does the equine breeding season start and finish in the northern hemisphere?

ITQ 12 List three natural factors that trigger the first of the hormonal changes at the start of the breeding season:

1.

2.

3.

ITQ 13

a. What is the term used to describe the period outside the breeding season, i.e. when there is no ovarian activity?

b. Give two names for the period between the last day of one heat and the first day of the next.

c. What is the normal duration of the period described at b.?

ITQ 14 What is the usual length of the whole oestrus cycle?

ITQ 15 Name the different types of hormone releasing factors and state their primary roles in the oestrus cycle.

ITQ 16 Match the stage of the oestrus cycle with the relevant description below.

Stages of the oestrus cycle:
1. Oestrus.
2. Dioestrus.
3. Anoestrus.

Descriptions:
1. The months between the breeding seasons where the length of day is short and the mare cannot conceive (from September/October through to February/March). The mare shows no interest in the stallion.

2. Five to six days when the mare is receptive to the stallion's advances.

3. The fifteen to sixteen days that form the period where the follicle is maturing before the egg is released. The mare shows no interest in the stallion.

ITQ 17 What behavioural response is likely to be performed by a sexually receptive mare?

In pregnancy, changes in hormone production bring about behavioural changes. Typically, the mare becomes calmer but increasingly defensive towards other horses, particularly male horses.

The mare's behaviour within the herd may change to some degree depending on her rank and social group. Most of the pregnant mare's time is spent with her family members and she may also begin to spend more time with other pregnant mares as they feed in the same areas. Higher ranking mares, particularly the lead mare, may take a less proactive role in directing and orientating the herd's movements and may be less physically able to maintain her position at the front whilst the herd is roaming as her pregnancy progresses.

The Sexual Behaviour of the Stallion

The sexual characteristics and behaviour of the stallion are largely influenced by the hormone **testosterone**. Testosterone is responsible for sperm production, foetal reproductive organ development, the changes that occur during puberty such as the descent of the testicles, and the stallion's sexual drive.

Some of the effects of testosterone actually occur before the birth of the foal in order for the male genitalia to develop and for important testosterone-induced changes in the brain to be established. However, the presence of the testes ensure continued testosterone production as the colt matures, and leads to further behavioural and physiological changes in the following years of life, e.g. the onset of sexual behaviour.

Interestingly, testosterone levels are also influenced by the length of daylight. During the winter months stallions tend not to demonstrate a strong sex drive in the way they behave, despite the fact that they are physiologically fertile. However, in the spring they begin to undergo physical changes associated with testosterone, such as developing a well-crested neck, increased bodyweight, increased muscular definition and generally behaving in a more 'stallion-like' way.

In general, the sexual behaviour of the stallion can be divided into two main components:

- maintaining and protecting the structure of the harem
- courtship and mating behaviour.

The way in which these behaviours are performed varies considerably with the stallion's age and previous experience.

The Maintenance and Protection of the Harem

Within the herd's structure, the stallion adopts the responsibility of ensuring that herd members remain grouped together and that no intruders or other stallions disrupt this balance. The best location from which the stallion can monitor the herd is from the back – he will engage in various forms of behaviour which enable him to maintain the herd, including a **snaking manoeuvre** whereby he lowers and lengthens the head and neck with his ears flat back. As the stallion moves behind or alongside the other horses, he swings his head from side to side to help drive the herd forward, to keep the mares grouped or to drive a rival stallion away. He may also patrol the edges of the grazing or resting herd.

If a rival stallion confronts the harem stallion a series of aggressive threats may be performed, including foot stamping and rearing. However, it is important for the stallion to avoid direct conflict and the unnecessary waste of energy.

Courtship and Mating Behaviour

When a mare is coming into oestrus, the stallion can detect this and begins to show interest in her. Different stallions have been observed in the wild to have individual preferences in the type of mare they pursue and many suggest this to be governed by the colour of the mare's coat.

Initial behaviour will involve the stallion approaching the mare with an elevated gait and posture, which serves to attract her attention and interest. This will also incorporate vocalizations (nickers and whinnies), snaking manoeuvres and playful biting of the mare's rump. This behaviour is shown over the course of several days.

The mare may initially respond with threats, using her hind legs to kick out at the stallion, who will retreat then continue to circle her and display until her aggressive signals stop. If the mare is in full oestrus however, she tolerates such behaviour and allows him to court her further. From this point he will begin to smell her more closely from her muzzle to the region of her **perineum** (area under the tail). The mare may become more responsive and adopt the braced stance described earlier, whilst raising her tail to emphasize vulval 'winking'. This encourages the stallion to further investigate the secretions in the perineal area, to which he responds with the **Flehmen** response, extending his head and neck and curling back his upper lip. At this stage the stallion's increased arousal level causes his penis to extend and become erect.

Copulation then follows. The stallion will be ready to cover a mare again only ten minutes after copulation and, in total, a harem stallion may cover the same mare up to ten times. In the days following copulation, the stallion will make a concerted effort to direct more attention than usual to the covered mares, ensuring that no other stallions can court them.

ITQ 18 Name the male sex hormone that influences the sexual and reproductive development and behaviour of the stallion.

ITQ 19 How does the stallion keep the herd group together?

FEEDING BEHAVIOUR

The anatomy and physiology of the horse's digestive system have evolved to allow the horse to ingest and digest substantial amounts of high fibre roughage effectively. The horse's stomach is relatively small and, as it cannot hold a great quantity of food, the horse has to spend a large proportion of the day feeding in order to ingest the required amounts. Hence the horse is termed a '**trickle feeder**', eating little and often whilst on the move, and resulting in the stomach being about half full at any one time.

The horse's feeding behaviour includes both grazing and browsing of trees and shrubs according to the type of vegetation that is available. Although grass is often the most readily available form of vegetation, horses will also consume fruit, tree bark and seaweed. Taste and smell are thought to play a large part in the horse's selection of vegetation, allowing the horse to use his upper lip to either select or reject different blades of grass. This in turn enables horses to avoid poisonous plants and can also ensure the selection of vegetation with the optimum nutritional value. For example, the horse tends to prefer the varieties of grasses that are more succulent and of better quality. Indeed, horses will avoid grazing in the area surrounding dung piles, whether they are their own or those of another horse.

Feral horses have been observed to spend between 60 and 70 per cent of each day grazing (that is between 14 and 17 hours of a 24-hour period). However, where there is little grazing available, the horse will have to invest more time in obtaining his daily requirements. This may be the case in more arid conditions with less vegetation or during winter when the horse has to paw with his front hooves to find grass beneath the snow.

Episodes of grazing can last from half an hour to several hours, depending on the movement of the herd. Feral horses also tend to feed according to the time of day, with grazing peaking during the early morning and late afternoon. However, horses may also graze well into the night.

DRINKING

The drinking behaviour of the feral horse varies according to the availability of water sources, the temperature of the surrounding environment and relevant individual factors such as bodyweight, breed and gender). The horse drinks by lowering his lips into the water, sucking and swallowing regularly. While this gentle sucking action does not disturb the underlayer of a muddy watering hole, it is safer to avoid allowing our domesticated horses to drink from streams with a sandy base. The total amount of water that a horse is thought to consume each day equates to approximately 36 litres (8 gallons), although this is a very broad average figure, given the range of equine sizes, climatic variations, exertion, etc.)

In a typical bout of drinking the horse ingests approximately 4.5 litres (1 gallon) of water. However, the horse will regularly raise his head and neck in order to survey the area for danger as, in the wild, watering holes are a common hunting ground for hungry predators. The distance to the nearest watering hole can vary considerably, meaning that the horse must remain adaptable in his drinking behaviour. In feral conditions, if a herd is grazing near a watering hole, the horses may take regular drinks throughout the day. However, if the grazing site is situated a long distance from a watering hole, the herd may only venture there to take one drink in the day.

The order in which different horses drink from a watering hole gives an indication of the social structure and dominance hierarchy of the herd. The dominant herd members (e.g. the stallion) tend to drink first, even if they are the last to arrive on site. In survival terms, this means that the more dominant members have a higher chance of ingesting a desirable quantity of water. More subordinate members, on the other hand, must wait their turn and drink what may be the limited remains of leftover water from the bottom of the hole, particularly if conditions are dry. This also avoids unnecessary conflict between competing herd members every time the herd drinks from a watering hole.

Different herds tend not to drink from the same source at the same time as this inevitably results in conflict between unfamiliar horses, particularly among competing stallions. However, such meetings may not occur that frequently because of the horse's reluctance to drink water from an unfamiliar source.

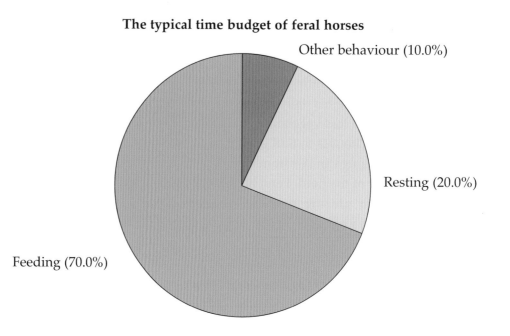

The typical time budget of feral horses

Other behaviour (10.0%)

Resting (20.0%)

Feeding (70.0%)

- Resting behaviour includes standing (15%) and lying (5%)
- Other behaviour refers to eliminative behaviour, grooming and play

Figure 3 The percentage of time that feral horses perform different maintenance behaviours

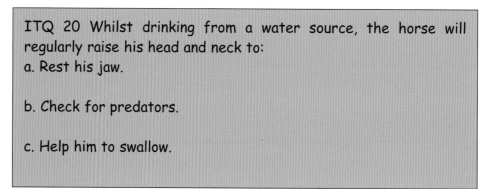

ITQ 20 Whilst drinking from a water source, the horse will regularly raise his head and neck to:
a. Rest his jaw.

b. Check for predators.

c. Help him to swallow.

RESTING

When the horse is resting, he may either remain standing or he may lie down. The resting behaviour of the horse involves not just sleeping, but also being drowsy or inactive (in effect the horse is resting without falling asleep). However, we will look at sleeping first.

Sleeping

The horse sleeps for approximately seven hours of every day, although, as with many other behaviours, sleeping is performed in bouts. However, the factors associated with the horse's environment and diet, and individual characteristics such as age, will influence the duration and quality of the sleep achieved. Younger horses sleep for slightly longer and spend proportionally more of this time sleeping flat on their sides (in **lateral recumbency**) than older horses. Horses often sleep lying down but in a basically upright position (in **sternal recumbency**), and can often be seen resting their muzzle on the ground.

While younger horses need more sleep than adults in order to grow and develop properly, they can also be protected and forewarned of danger by older herd members. Each adult herd member will take their turn at being 'on guard for danger' on behalf of the rest of the herd, the majority of whom may be sleeping at the same time. Older herd members must also look after themselves and therefore tend to sleep standing up. The horse has undoubtedly evolved anatomically and physiologically (witness the 'stay apparatus' of the upper hind limbs) to allow him to sleep while standing up. This is adaptive behaviour, since the horse is vulnerable to predators or other dangers when lying asleep on the ground. If standing, the horse can quickly escape from predators if the situation demands.

This ability notwithstanding, the actual quality of sleep is somewhat dependent on the horse's physical position. When lying down, the horse may enter the deeper stages of sleep. Researchers believe that, if the horse reaches the rapid eye movement stage of sleep (**REM sleep**), he may experience dreaming sensations similar to those of humans. However, it is not possible for a horse who is sleeping standing up to reach this deep stage of sleep.

Wakeful Resting

During the summer months the horse may not have to invest as much energy as usual in obtaining good quality grazing and may therefore spend more time either resting in the shade or loafing in the sun whilst half dozing off. It is unlikely that the horse will be able to spend time loafing if his feeding, watering and social needs have not been fulfilled. As the horse will have to work much harder to find food in the winter months, there may be less time available for such resting behaviour.

ITQ 21 List four factors that affect both the quality and number of hours of sleep gained by horses in the wild.

ELIMINATIVE BEHAVIOUR

The term eliminative behaviour refers to the different ways in which the horse expels waste products from his body, namely through the passing of droppings (dunging) and urination.

Dunging

Dunging behaviour varies according to a number of factors. The 'typical' horse will pass 10–15 droppings a day at intervals of approximately 2½–4 hours. However, stallions tend to pass droppings in piles and will deliberately do so over other horses' dung piles after having spent some time smelling them. Indeed, the stallion may turn around and smell the pile again after having added his contribution. In addition to this the stallion may pass droppings around the boundaries of his territory in order to deter potential intruders. Mares, however, pay less attention to where they pass droppings, although they do tend to pass droppings in response to smelling those of other horses. Dung piles may also serve the function of helping herd members to orientate themselves.

Urination

The way in which the horse urinates depends in particular on the gender of the horse. All horses will adopt a straddled stance prior to and during urination, whilst also attempting to position themselves so as not to splash their legs by avoiding urinating on hard ground. Neither mares nor stallions are able to urinate whilst on the move. The mare generally tends to pass urine once in approximately every four hours, but this frequency can increase greatly when she is in season, accompanied by her straddled posture and other elements of reproductive behaviour.

The mare may also urinate in response to smelling another horse's droppings. However, a stallion will make the effort to urinate directly over another horse's dung, particularly that of a mare. These actions are thought to assist the stallion in hiding the reproductive status of the mare from other stallions and to inform other horses that the mare is already being escorted by him.

ITQ 22 In what ways does the eliminative behaviour of the stallion differ from that of the mare?

GROOMING

In the wild, horses are exposed to large numbers of different skin parasites (flies, ticks, lice, etc.). Therefore self-grooming, using the teeth to nibble the skin, and rubbing various body parts on other objects such as trees, can help to reduce parasite infestations whilst also relieving any itching sensations and increasing blood circulation.

Additionally, grooming during the summer months may help to dislodge moulting hair, dead skin and dried sweat or mud, whilst also helping to stimulate the secretion of natural oils through the coat, which provide protection from water. Grooming also forms the basis of important elements of the herd's social behaviour. Two horses may simultaneously groom each other and therefore allow body regions that each horse cannot reach themselves to be attended to. This process of mutual-grooming (also known as **allogrooming**) may be used by horses unfamiliar with each other when attempting to become acquainted, and is also a way of maintaining a pre-established bond between certain herd members.

Figure 4 Mutual grooming

This mutual grooming is particularly common between mare and foal and between preferred grooming partners. These latter are sometimes referred to as **pair bonds** – that is, the horses that certain herd members choose to spend most of their time with or in close proximity to.

In addition to the forms of grooming mentioned, other activities that serve similar functions involve shaking and swishing the tail and also rolling. Rolling on dry ground may also help to dry the horse's coat when wet from water or sweat.

Although grooming is essential, the frequency with which it is performed will vary according to whether the horse has fulfilled his need for food and water, and the proportion of the day that must be allocated to these activities.

ITQ 23
a. What are the two different forms of grooming that a horse may engage in?

b. List the purpose and function of both forms of grooming.

COMMUNICATION

In order to survive and reproduce effectively in the wild, horses have evolved with a highly intricate communication system which enables the social structure of the herd and its social dynamics to remain relatively organized and stable. Additionally, the senses that act as the medium for social behaviour among horses are also the senses that facilitate the behavioural adaptations that promote survival.

The main channels of communication (**message channels**) adopted by the horse involve the senses of sight, hearing and **chemoreception,** the last of which can be further subdivided into smell (**olfaction**) and taste (**gustation**). These components can be combined to communicate a seemingly simple message (e.g. when a horse attempts to communicate his location to other horses) but can also be used when dealing with far more complex situations (e.g. when a stallion demonstrates his ownership of the harem to an approaching unfamiliar horse). In all circumstances where information is successfully communicated between different individuals, there will always be a **communicator** (the horse who generates the information or message) and a **recipient** (the horse who receives and interprets the message that has been communicated).

Throughout evolution, certain mutations in the horse's behaviour, physiology and anatomy will have been favoured for the role they play in the horse's communication system. (For example, horses who vocalized more often than other horses may have been more successful when attempting to attract a mating partner.) However, the specific mutations that were favoured throughout evolution have, in part, also been selected according to the ability of each horse to display, recognize and interpret communicative signals. (Thus it is only advantageous for a horse seeking a mate to vocalize more often if other horses of the opposite gender pay attention to such behaviour.) In essence, it is highly desirable that each herd member is equally skilled at fulfilling both roles of communicator and recipient. It is likely that the type of behavioural, physiological and anatomical mutations that other horses tend to pay attention to (or prefer), offer information about the genetic fitness of the communicator. This mechanism allows the feral horse to select prospective mating partners – for a mare to recognize when a particular stallion is stronger and more likely to win a conflict, for example.

Additionally, communicative behaviour that may be favoured in one environment may not be elsewhere. For example, vocal signals may be more effective in an environment where horses cannot see each other very well (like a forest). Alternatively, in a desert environment, herd members can read each other's body language more effectively and may vocalize to a lesser extent. Overall, the mutations that have been favoured historically for the ways in which they assist equine communication have evolved through a combination of genetic predisposition, learning through experience and environmental pressures.

ITQ 24 What are the three main factors that shape the communicative behaviour of horses?

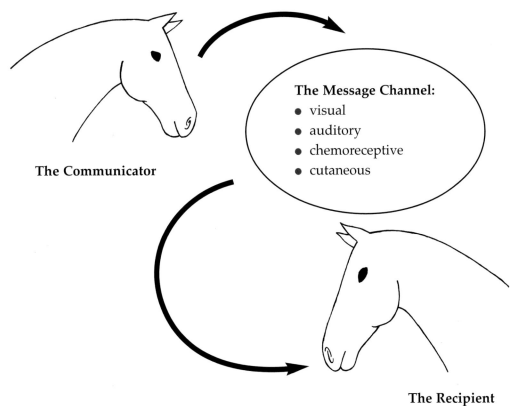

The Communicator

The Message Channel:
- visual
- auditory
- chemoreceptive
- cutaneous

The Recipient

Figure 5 How information may be transferred between horses

SOCIAL BEHAVIOUR OF THE HERD
The Home Range

Every herd has its own geographical area of land within which it roams (the **home range**). This can stretch from 1–50 square kilometres (0.4–19 square miles) in size. The size is largely determined by the availability of resources, such as watering holes, grazing sites and shelter from adverse weather conditions and insects. Furthermore, a herd makes seasonal movements within a home range and therefore preserves some areas at certain times of the year.

In fact the climate and type of land that the herd occupies have strong influences upon the way that the herd behaves. It is usual for the home ranges of different herds to overlap, which may prove a source of conflict during the mating season or when certain resources (e.g. food or water) become limited.

In wetter climates home ranges tend to be smaller in size because of the greater availability of food and water resources. However, if the population density is particularly high, stallions may be compelled to defend their territory despite ample resources. Bands that occupy marshland form large herds whilst engaging in various forms of resting behaviour in the summer; this is believed to reduce the incidence of being bitten by flies. This pattern diminishes during the winter months.

Where more than one herd shares a resource, a watering hole for example, the largest herd appears to gain primary access. Under such circumstances, the herd stallions ensure that each herd remains formed.

Herd Structure

A herd can be described as an ordered social unit, which is composed of groups of horses (either **harems** or **bands**) that adopt similar patterns of movement within a communal home range. The overall size of the herd depends on both the number of horses in the geographical area (the **population density**) and the availability and quality of resources (food, shelter, water) necessary for survival. Depending on circumstances, herd numbers can range from as few as five, through typical figures in the mid-teens to considerably greater numbers.

In order for the social environment of the herd to remain relatively stable, and therefore for the individuals to survive and reproduce, the herd members must be able to:

– recognize other herd members effectively
– coordinate different survival behaviours efficiently
– successfully develop and maintain social bonds.

Different social groups and social roles exist within a single herd. If herd members fail to maintain these social groups and roles, the occurrence of aggressive behaviour will increase and the social structure of the herd is likely to change. A specific social group of horses is referred to as a **band**. Indeed, several different bands of horses may be found within one herd.

Family bands consist of several mares, their offspring under three years of age and at least one mature stallion. The mares tend to develop extremely strong social bonds with their foals, but can also do so with other mares with whom they have been raised when young, particularly siblings. Where more than one stallion exists in a family group, the dominant stallion has supreme mating rights, which is one reason why he allows his fellow stallions to stay. Those immature stallions aged above two years of age who challenge the dominant stallion unsuccessfully might then group together to form a **bachelor band**. The bachelor band will leave the herd and remain as a band until they are successful in their search for a harem herd. All the members of a bachelor band will be sexually mature. Activities such as mutual grooming and play-fighting will be evident in the band, which help to prime and develop each stallion's ability to negotiate or win rights over harems in the future. In general, the number of stallions in a bachelor band can range from three to eight. However, certain stallions may be unsuccessful at joining a bachelor group and may roam alone, until they come across a lone mare.

A **harem** exists as a group of mares that roams within a home range without a harem stallion. However, a harem is unlikely to remain 'stallion-free' for a prolonged length of time and is therefore quite rare in feral conditions.

Social Roles of Herd Members

Within the social environment, different herd members have different relationships among themselves, which not only affect the social structure of the herd but also shape the roles that different herd members adopt.

It is most common for a herd to have one **lead or Alpha mare**. She is likely to be the individual most familiar with the surrounding environment and how to navigate within it, and also adept in the various skills of survival.

Typically, a herd will also have a dominant stallion, whose role it is to keep the herd together and to defend his mares. When herd members stray over a certain distance from the herd, the stallion engages in a 'snaking' manoeuvre that rounds up the individuals and directs them back towards the herd. For this reason, the stallion remains at the back of the herd as it roams. This ensures that he can view the entire harem in front of him and round up those members who may lag behind or wander. Thus the stallion patrols the periphery of the herd whilst they graze or rest.

It is also the role of the stallion to keep other stallions or intruders from coming close to his mares and their foals by moving his herd away from them. Where a herd's home range overlaps with that of another, the stallion will have to invest more energy in defending his mares. This may entail fighting between stallions, which starts with a series of threats when rearing will occur. This allows each stallion to size up the other one, and may determine the victor without escalating into further violence and injury.

Other roles which exist within the herd may not be adopted by just one individual herd member. For example, there seems to be an instinctive understanding that there needs to be a horse on the lookout for danger. In effect, different herd members may take turns in fulfilling this role, so that all get a chance to graze, roll, etc.

Additionally, certain herd members can influence various forms of behaviour by other herd members. For example, if one horse begins to flee an area, for example, others may almost instantaneously engage in the same behaviour. Alternatively, one horse could start to roll on the ground and, on seeing this, others may begin to do the same.

This process whereby one horse is more likely to perform certain behaviour after seeing another horse do so is called **social facilitation**. However, certain herd members may be more influential in this respect than others. For example, herd members are less likely to engage in a fleeing response if a young foal starts to run. However, if it were either the stallion or lead mare, other herd members would be far more likely to react. The same is true of individuals who hold closer social bonds, demonstrating that horses will pay more notice to the behaviour of certain individuals as compared to other herd members.

ITQ 25 Complete the sentences.

A group of horses that lives in the wild as a stable and organized structure is referred to as a...................... The area of land that the herd tends to roam and survive in is called the ....and can stretch up to........................... This area varies in size according to the availability of resources such as ...., ... and................ Within the herd, smaller social groups of horses are referred to as a..........................., which consists of several mares, their foals, and a stallion. Where several sexually mature stallions form a group together, this is termed a ....

Social Rank within the Herd Hierarchy

Within a stable herd, certain individuals will repeatedly dominate other individuals in conflict situations. For example, certain herd members will always successfully fend off other herd members from a favoured area of shelter or grazing. The consistency with which this occurs allows each horse to gain a rank that reflects their position in the herd relative to the other horses. As the rank of each member of a herd remains relatively constant, the herd is said to have a **dominance hierarchy** (also known as a 'pecking order'). However, as different herd members have different roles in different situations, it is unlikely that a horse can have one rank within the hierarchy across all the different situations that arise. A good example of this would be how the persistent sequence in which the herd members take a drink from a watering hole does not correspond with the order by which herd members take turns in monitoring the environment for predators, or are entitled to food resources. Thus, this hierarchy may not be **linear**: a horse who is ranked number five in a herd may generally precede the horse ranked number ten, but may be subordinate to a horse ranked number seven in certain situations. Interestingly, when a mare has a foal at foot, her rank may increase temporarily as she becomes particularly protective of her offspring.

The larger the herd size, the more complex (less linear) the dominance hierarchy. Overall, the lead mare and stallion share the number one rank in the herd depending on the situation. For example, the mare will decide in which direction the herd travels and the stallion will follow the herd. However, the lead mare may take more of a back-seat role while the stallion is protecting the herd from a rival stallion.

Several factors are believed to determine where an individual horse fits into the overall hierarchy. These include age, size, motivation and experience. (Younger herd members are generally lower ranking.) However, research suggests that a horse's rank may be genetically determined to a certain extent. Indeed, the foals of higher-ranking mares appear to adopt a similar rank within their own peer group as they mature and progress through to adulthood. However, a foal may also learn the behavioural tendencies that determine rank from his mother's behaviour, which suggests that a horse's rank can develop and be established through a combination of genetic predispositions and learning from experience within a given environment.

ITQ 26 Sort out which responsibilities are those of the lead mare and which are those of the stallion from the list below.

- Keeping the herd together.

- Remaining at the back of the herd.

- Allocation of resources.

- Navigation and orientation of the home range.

- Defending the herd from intruders.

ITQ 27 What is 'social facilitation' ?

ITQ 28 What do we mean when we speak of a horse's 'social rank' ?

A dominance hierarchy may be established over the space of two days but will undergo adjustment every time an individual horse either joins or leaves the herd. With consistency, it is possible for each herd member to acknowledge those other herd members who can be challenged successfully and those who should not be interfered with. The purpose of this dominance hierarchy is to avoid the need for constant conflict over resources that would occur in a group-living species that had no hierarchy. In effect, marginal aggression in the short term serves to reduce the prospect of prolonged or incessant aggression, which would demand a great deal of energy and time.

Importantly, the social hierarchy is not maintained purely through dominance relationships: **tolerance** is also a major factor. Highly ranked herd members will have a degree of preference for other herd members, depending on their rank. This network of tolerance functions as a chain down through the hierarchical system. Each horse's tolerance of or preference for particular herd members is usually indicated by the degree to which two horses follow one another, and stand and interact together in a reciprocal manner.

Tolerance, as a trait, is evident in the general attitude of mature horses to the young members of the herd, who are given the opportunity to mix with other members of their own species. In some circumstance, this tolerance can be heightened to the level of overt protection, as, for example, when a mare fosters an orphan foal.

Interactive Behaviour
Aggressive Behaviour

As we have seen, having a dominance hierarchy helps the social organization of the herd to remain stable, so that each herd member can invest their energy towards behaviour that promotes survival without wasting energy on repeated aggressive conflicts. By avoiding aggressive interactions, herd members also reduce the potential risks that are associated with fighting, such as serious injury or separation from the herd. Overall, the less frequently aggressive interactions occur within a herd, the better that herd members are at developing and maintaining social bonds, herd structure and social cohesion.

Affiliative Behaviour

Horses spend the greater part of their time engaging in **affiliative** (more friendly) behaviour. However, relatively little research has been focused upon the types of visual signals and postural changes that are used during such interactions between herd members. Some clear examples of the signals that reflect such interaction include mutual grooming, social play and pair bonds remaining within a close proximity to each other throughout the day as grazing neighbours.

As with aggressive behaviour, affiliative behaviour serves to develop and maintain social bonds, herd structure and social cohesion, therefore helping to ensure the survival of the herd. It is claimed that the strong social relationships between mares plays a major part in the overall cohesion of the herd.

Play Behaviour

Play behaviour is most marked amongst foals and juvenile horses. Such interactions are characterized by running, leaping, the manipulation of objects and performing elements of adult fighting and reproductive behaviour patterns. However, play behaviour differs according to the gender and age of the horse. Fillies engage in more active forms of play (e.g. fast running) and exaggerated postures. Colts, on the other hand, adopt more interactive play (involving more physical contact) with other colts. The functions of play behaviour that are commonly proposed emphasize the role it serves in the development of neuromuscular fitness of the young horse's body, as well as the horse's learning abilities and social relationships.

Changes in Herd Structure

A herd will inevitably encounter various changes in its structure. The most obvious changes occur when either existing herd members die or new herd members are born. Other than this, changes within a herd occur through the dispersal of young horses from one maternal group to another. Additionally, young mares and colts will leave their natal herd and move to new breeding grounds on reaching sexual maturity. In such circumstances the young mares are usually abducted by a stallion or ousted by elder mares of the herd. Young mares may, however, leave a herd voluntarily if there is a particularly high population density of their peer group. Young males are more inclined to leave the herd voluntarily regardless of group numbers. Sometimes, however, the dominant stallion may also force the young males away following the arrival of new offspring.

ADVANTAGES AND DISADVANTAGES OF HERD SOCIETY
Advantages

The highly organized social structure of the herd functions to maximize each herd member's chances of survival and reproductive success. However, the survival aspect does not, generally, encompass the aspect of finding food. In the wild, the type of food that the horse eats will, in normal circumstances, be distributed over a relatively large area and herd living will have little impact on the ability of horses to find it. There is also little cause for horses in a herd to compete over food resources in the way that other species may have to. In effect, the horses can remain as a social group without compromising each individual's required nutritional intake. When necessary, however, one advantage of living in a group is that a herd is better able than individuals to defend their resources such as grazing sites, watering holes and shelter. When food resources do become limited, the herd may adapt by dividing itself up into smaller groups in order to forage more successfully.

A major factor in the enhancement of survival prospects is that herd living offers supreme protection from predators. In a herd, there are many pairs of eyes to survey the surrounding environment and warn the rest of the herd as appropriate. Statistically, in the event of an attack, any individual is less likely to fall victim to a predator if part of a herd (particularly a large one) than if living in isolation. Added to this, herd members together stand a better chance of driving away a predator or creating confusing conditions for the predators by their fleeing behaviour.

Disadvantages

However, there are undesirable consequences associated with social living among herd members. Certain adverse conditions may necessitate abnormal competition over limited resources, with a correspondingly increased risk of sustaining serious injury. The likelihood of contracting infectious diseases (and, in some circumstances, other illnesses) may increase as a result of interactions with other herd members. Despite these drawbacks, however, feral horses remain a social species, which indicates that the advantages outweigh the disadvantages of doing so.

CHAPTER SUMMARY

Whether you are a one-horse owner or manager of several horses, recognition of good and ill health in the horse is essential. In addition to an appreciation of his physiological well-being, it is important to consider the horse's psychological well-being – this is where an understanding of the horse's natural behaviour is valuable. In this chapter we have introduced the principles of equine behaviour, discussing how feral horses behave within the herd. While our horses are no longer feral, they retain the same instincts, and this should be taken into account when caring for them.

Fortunately, equine behavioural science is an emerging field, with an increasing awareness the of horses' behavioural and psychological needs.

CHAPTER 2

ROUTINE HEALTH CARE

The aims and objectives of this chapter are to explain:

- The 'five freedoms' that should be applied to horse management.
- The daily aspects of routine care that contribute to provision of the 'five freedoms'.
- Why horses need shoeing and what the shoeing process involves.
- The ways in which internal parasites affect the horse's health.
- The life cycles of the most common species of worm that infect horses.
- How to control worm infestation.
- When and why horses need to have their teeth rasped.
- Which vaccinations are needed to maintain health.

THE FIVE FREEDOMS

In 1992, the Farm Animal Welfare Council developed a set of major criteria that were considered to typify the way in which the welfare of farmed animals needed to be monitored and regulated, and to guide pieces of legislation relating to animal welfare. While, under various legal definitions, horses do not seem to be 'farm animals', the 'five freedoms' identified provide a straightforward means through which the welfare of any animal can be examined in terms of the physiological and behavioural needs of the species concerned (see Table 2).

Through developments in all areas of equine science, particularly that of behavioural science, experts are now more able to evaluate the extent to which modern management and training practices embraced by the equine industry accommodate the 'five freedoms'. Indeed, before advances in behavioural science emerged, we knew more about the horse's physical requirements than their behavioural needs. By considering how most horses are managed today it is clear that many practices do not grant horses the 'five freedoms'. The majority of horses are stabled individually compared to being group housed in barns. Some horses never have access to turnout. Many horses are weaned abruptly and 'broken in' in an unsympathetic manner.

Despite the advances in equine science, there are many areas that need to be researched in order for certain issues relating to equine welfare to be better understood. For example, little scientific research has focused on the reliable assessment of pain in horses. As a prey species the horse has evolved to stoically mask symptoms of pain in order to avoid being singled out by predators. Hence we may not be as good at spotting pain in horses as we would wish.

The 'Five Freedoms'	Equine Examples
1. Freedom from hunger, thirst and malnutrition	<ul><li>Balanced diet suited to the needs of the individual horse.</li><li>Adequate roughage.</li><li>High quality feedstuffs.</li><li>Provision of regular small meals.</li><li>Ad lib supply of fresh and clean water. When this is not possible, water should be offered regularly.</li><li>Regular and skilful dental care.</li></ul>
2. Freedom from physical and thermal discomfort	<ul><li>Good stable design.</li><li>Absence of draughts.</li><li>Effective ventilation and insulation in loose boxes and whilst in transit.</li><li>Provision of good quality bedding material.</li><li>Provision of well-fitting rugs when clipped or turned out in bad weather.</li><li>Provision of shelter and/or windbreaks in paddocks.</li><li>Suitable fittening programme allowing horse to compete safely in his discipline.</li><li>Acclimatization period when competing in foreign climates.</li><li>Adequate rest.</li></ul>
3. Freedom from pain, injury and disease	<ul><li>Regular exercise.</li><li>Adequate ventilation.</li><li>Good quality feed and bedding.</li><li>Avoidance of overfeeding.</li><li>Maintenance of a clean bed.</li><li>No sharp or uneven surfaces in horse's environment.</li><li>Routine vaccinations.</li><li>Considerate riding using well-fitted and appropriate tack.</li><li>Appropriate fittening programme.</li><li>Regular worming, skilful shoeing and dental care.</li><li>Timely veterinary consultation and appropriate medical treatment.</li><li>Timely euthanasia.</li></ul>
4. Freedom from fear and distress	<ul><li>No overcrowding or total isolation.</li><li>Humane handling and training methods.</li><li>Horse's confidence and ability built by training appropriately, in accordance to the horse's role.</li><li>Humane transportation conditions.</li><li>Humane weaning methods.</li><li>No physical prevention of abnormal behaviour (stable vices).</li><li>Humane euthanasia.</li></ul>
5. Freedom to express most normal patterns of behaviour	<ul><li>Ability to express foraging behaviour.</li><li>Opportunities for social interaction, play and exploration.</li><li>Adequate space for roaming and exercise.</li><li>Normal sexual and reproductive behaviour.</li></ul>

Table 2 The 'five freedoms'

It may be difficult to weigh up the importance of certain welfare concerns when the fulfilment of a particular welfare standard prevents a different welfare standard from being upheld. For example, clipping a horse's coat may be necessary to keep the horse free from thermal discomfort during exercise in the winter, but the clipping procedure may not permit the horse freedom from fear and distress. Alternatively, the provision of straw bedding has been linked with a reduction in the incidence of abnormal behaviour but at the same time it may cause colic and/or increase the intensity of respiratory disorders in certain horses.

However, although the 'five freedoms' serve an important purpose of allowing us to monitor the welfare of horses in domestic conditions, it should be understood that they represent an ideal to which we should aspire as far as possible, rather than a total practicality. In this respect, total adherence to these ideals is also impossible for horses living in feral conditions – there is no guarantee that they will remain free from pain, hunger, fear, etc. With the domesticated horse, the aim is to strike a balance in which these freedoms are impinged upon as little as possible.

THE FIVE FREEDOMS AND DAILY MANAGEMENT

As daily management probably has the greatest impact on his psychological and physical well-being, the 'five freedoms' can be used as a basis for evaluating the horse's daily routine.

Freedom from Hunger, Thirst and Malnutrition

Although feeding is covered in greater depth in the following chapters, it warrants a mention here. Feeding and the feeding regime can influence the horse's health to a great extent. The horse is intended to be a 'trickle feeder', eating small quantities of high-fibre food over a prolonged period. Giving the horse plenty of hay mimics what nature intended and keeps the horse occupied both physically and mentally. All food, including hay, should be of good quality – don't make false economies by feeding poor quality food as the horse's health can be affected.

Always bear in mind the very important rule of feeding according to type, temperament and the work to be done and to feed 'little and often'. Small, regular feeds help to reduce boredom.

All horses should receive a balanced diet, suited to their individual needs. Consider also that overfeeding often has worse consequences for horses than underfeeding. Laminitis is an extremely painful condition which, among its many causes, can be numbered overfeeding starchy feeds or allowing unrestricted access to lush grass. So, while one freedom, the freedom from hunger, is satisfied, such practices take away another freedom – the freedom from pain.

There must be a constant supply of fresh, clean water. In any circumstances where this is not possible, e.g. on a long journey, water should be offered regularly, i.e. at approximately two-hourly intervals and more frequently in hot weather.

Freedom from Physical and Thermal Discomfort

There are many factors which can cause physical discomfort. For example poorly designed stables (too small, ceilings too low for example), ill-fitting tack or rugs, etc.

Thermal discomfort can be caused by being either too hot or too cold. The stable or shelter must be well ventilated but draught-proof. In the stable, never try to keep the horse warm by restricting fresh air – the top door should be open at all times. Stale air in a stable is unhealthy as it can harbour airborne infections and dust spores. Ammonia from the urine can build up, which is harmful to the respiratory system. Similarly, horses in transit must have appropriate rugs and adequate ventilation.

In warm weather, rugs on stabled or grass-kept horses must be changed or removed as appropriate. Horses at grass in hot weather need shade. Alternatively, protection from the cold, wind and rain must be provided through the use of windbreaks, shelter and/or rugs.

Bedding in a field shelter is optional – most horses are happy to lie directly on earth or grass.

Competition horses must be fittened to the correct level in order that they can compete without undue fatigue and distress. This includes allowing horses competing abroad or in extreme weather conditions to become acclimatized to unfamiliar conditions. At its extreme level, this may entail a prolonged period of acclimatization and expert advice and support.

Fatigue can cause discomfort so horses in regular hard work must be allowed time to rest and relax either in the field or stable. If stabled, allow the horses at least two or three hours during the daytime in which they can rest undisturbed. They soon learn to appreciate this routine and will feel happy to lie down during the rest period. Horses in hard work benefit from a break occasionally. This break maybe anything from a week to a couple of months and may be either total rest (turned out to grass), or simply a change in the type of work type – perhaps light hacking or some half-days with hounds instead of the usual workload. Hunters are traditionally rested in the summer, while eventers have a break over the winter.

Freedom from Pain, Injury and Disease

Timely consultation with the vet will do much to prevent and/or alleviate pain, injury and disease. By recognizing the signs of good and poor health you will be able to act promptly if something does go wrong. Prophylactic management (e.g. worming, vaccination, dental and hoof care) is also essential. Regular exercise provides stimulation and tones and conditions the musculoskeletal and cardiovascular systems. However, many horses suffer pain when ridden because of undiagnosed musculoskeletal injury, ill-fitting tack and inconsiderate riding. It is important to be on the lookout for signs of the first, as evidenced by factors such as gait irregularities, stiffness and tension; the second can be avoided with care and such expert advice as is necessary and the third is a matter of consideration and self-discipline.

With regard to musculoskeletal disorders, there are many horses who suffer from various forms of degenerative joint disease but who can still have a good quality of life through the administration of suitable analgesics and anti-inflammatory drugs. Likewise, there are many complementary therapies available which can help promote and restore normal function.

As mentioned earlier, overfeeding and unrestricted access to lush grass can cause laminitis in susceptible animals. This very painful condition may have long-lasting effects. Even animals who have never previously had laminitis should be considered as susceptible until their metabolic 'history' is well established and known to you. Unfortunately laminitis is a common condition, often caused inadvertently by the actions of well-meaning owners.

While a comfortable, well-managed retirement is a just reward for an old horse after years of service, timely euthanasia needs to be mentioned here. While understandably dreaded by most horse owners, it is ultimately our responsibility to make sure that our very old and/or chronically ill horses and ponies do not suffer by being allowed to linger for too many years, particularly if it is suspected that they are in pain.

Freedom from Fear and Distress

Separation from other herd members causes some horses a significant level of stress. However, this cannot always be avoided, as you will frequently need to separate your horse from his mates in order to ride or take him to a show. It is wrong to punish the horse for showing his anxiety – over time, with consistent, calm handling the horse should become more used to being separated. However, horses should never be kept permanently in isolation, neither should they be kept in overcrowded conditions.

Certain routine procedures cause fear and distress in some horses. Time, patience and skilful handling are needed to help nervous horses become accustomed to procedures such as clipping, shoeing and teeth rasping. Sometimes, for the horse's sake and for the handler and practitioner's safety, sedation is the most humane option. Horses should be consistently handled in a calm and confident manner – there is no place for rough or impatient handling.

Over-facing horses in competition or lack of preparation for competition can cause fear. Adequate and appropriate schooling and the development of the horse's confidence are essential.

Freedom to Express Most Normal Patterns of Behaviour

As discussed in Chapter 1, the horse is a herd animal with a natural instinct to wander and graze. There is always a danger that the stabled horse will become bored. Boredom is stressful to the horse and can lead to the development of repetitive so-called 'stable vices' (stereotypical behaviour) such as weaving and crib-biting.

If not living out permanently, horses should ideally be turned out for several hours a day and, whilst in the stable, should be able to look out and watch the comings and goings of the yard. Companionship is important so the horses can socialize – being herd animals, they should not be kept in complete isolation.

A constant supply of good quality hay in a net will help to keep the horse occupied and act as a substitute for foraging behaviour. Some horses appreciate 'toys' such as horseballs.

Unless used as a broodmare or for stallion duties, most domesticated horses do not get the chance to fully express sexual or reproductive behaviour. However, mixed sex groups (mares and geldings) turned out together will often show some forms of sexual interest, especially when the mares are in oestrus. The advantage of such groupings is that they mirror natural patterns; the potential disadvantage lies in the possibility of injuries from kicks, which, whilst a 'natural' risk, will not impress the owners of any recipients.

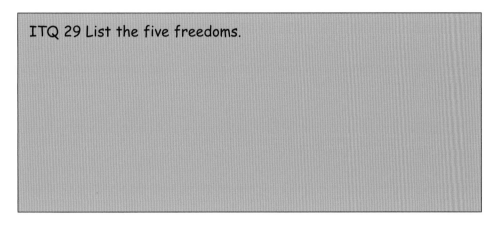

ITQ 29 List the five freedoms.

STABLING AND TURNING OUT

In light of the above we will now consider the pros and cons of stabling horses and turning horses out.

The Advantages of Stabling

- It enables food and water intake to be monitored. Controlling the intake of grass helps to prevent the horse from getting fat. It is also important if the horse or pony suffers from laminitis, when grass intake must be controlled in the growing seasons.

- Stabling provides protection against cold and wet in winter, heat, flies and midges in summer.

- By keeping the horse warmer he will not grow such a thick coat in winter, making him easier to groom.

- As the horse is protected from the elements he can be clipped and rugged, making it easier for him to work hard and maintain condition.

- It provides added security both against bullying by other horses and from thieves.

- It prevents paddocks from getting 'poached', i.e. churned up, in the winter.

- It is more convenient for the rider to get a stabled horse ready to ride.

ITQ 30 Without looking at the list below, what do you consider to be one of the main drawbacks of stabling horses for long periods?

The Disadvantages of Stabling for Long Periods

- The horse's natural instincts to wander, graze and socialize are denied so he may develop stereotypical behaviour to compensate.

- Boredom can result if the horse is stabled for long periods.

- The horse is unable to exercise himself and will need to be exercised every day.

- The horse may be more prone to dust allergies as he is in a confined area exposed to dust from hay and straw.

- It creates more work, e.g. mucking out, feeding, watering and exercising.

- There are additional costs, e.g. – bedding, hay and food.

The Advantages of Turning Out

- It alleviates boredom as the horse can wander and graze at liberty. The horse's natural desires to roam and graze are fulfilled, which helps to keep him mentally relaxed.

- He can act instinctively and socialize with other members of the 'herd'.

- The horse will be less prone to coughs, colds and dust allergies as he will be breathing fresh air constantly in a dust-free environment.

- The horse is able to exercise himself, so eliminating problems caused through insufficient exercise, such as filled legs, exertional rhabdomyolysis (azoturia) and general unruly behaviour.

- It saves labour as it reduces mucking out. Constant attention is not necessary.

- Money is saved on bedding materials, although a shelter should be provided if the horse lives out permanently and there is no natural shelter, e.g. hedges and trees. Bedding in a shelter is optional.

- Where necessary, grass intake can be restricted by confining the horse in a small fenced area and allowing the area to become over-grazed. This should be within sight and sound of other horses.

Figure 6 Domesticated horses turned out to grass

The Disadvantages of Turning Out

- There is a risk that the horse will sustain injury, either by galloping around or through being kicked by another horse. Horses should be turned out in small, compatible groups or in fields large enough to prevent dominant animals from bullying others.

- It is not possible to monitor the intake of grass, or water. In the spring and summer the horse may become overweight, possibly suffering from laminitis.

- If out permanently, the horse will develop a thick, greasy coat and will, particularly in winter, normally be very dirty, making it more difficult to prepare him for riding. If the horse has not been wearing a turnout rug and you wish to ride on a wet day, he will be wet and probably covered in mud.

- Unless a strict control and worming programme is adhered to, worm larvae are ingested so promoting the worms' life cycle and causing the spread of infestation. Droppings must therefore be picked up from the paddock very regularly in order to control worm infestations.

- It can be more difficult to maintain and monitor fitness.

- Wet mud around the legs can cause problems such as cracked heels and mud fever. The hooves also become softer if constantly wet so shoes should be worn to prevent the horse from becoming footsore.

- Wet, muddy turn-out rugs are difficult to handle and can be difficult to dry unless you have a heated rug room or large enough tack room in which to hang them.

- Changing rugs when turning out and bringing in is time-consuming.

- There is less security, especially if the field is away from the house or yard.

- Paddocks will become badly poached in wet weather. Gateways can be particularly bad.

Despite these 'disadvantages', it is important that all horses are turned out as much as is practicably possible – most horses are much healthier and more content when living out.

The Combined System

Keeping the horse partially stabled and partially out at grass enables one to enjoy the advantages of both systems. A balance can be struck – if a horse cannot live out permanently the ideal solution is to stable at night or in extreme bad weather, and turn out at all other times. In the summer, when the weather is very hot and flies are a problem, the horse may be stabled during the day and turned out at night. Alternatively, if the normal routine is adhered to, a shelter should be provided in the field.

ITQ 31 State the main advantage of allowing horses to spend time at grass.

PREVENTATIVE MANAGEMENT

We will now go on to look at various types of prophylactic (preventative) management – the things we do to protect our horses from injury and disease.

HOOF CARE
Routine Procedures

Regular attention from the farrier is essential. However, the hooves should also be cared for on a daily basis – they should be picked out at least once a day, preferably twice. This is to prevent a build-up of dirt and bacteria which could lead to the foul-smelling condition known as thrush. Picking the feet out regularly will also discover any stones that have become wedged in the foot, which can lead to a bruised sole and time off work.

The hoofpick and skip should be kept ready to hand and picking out the hooves should become automatic before tacking up, turning out and putting the horse back into the stable. Whilst picking out hooves, look for any signs that the horse may need re-shoeing and for signs of injury to the heels and sole. Puncture wounds can cause permanent damage and carry the risk of tetanus so you need to keep a lookout for damage to the sole.

If you feel so inclined, a coat of hoof oil daily keeps the hoof wall looking smart and may help temporarily to prevent the evaporation of moisture. In a busy yard however, there is often no time for the extra touches such as hoof oil. One school of thought suggests that hoof oil prevents the foot from absorbing moisture in wet conditions and so can contribute to brittle hooves in the long run. If the horse is prone to brittle hooves, there is a range of products on the market designed to 'moisturize' the hoof wall and improve the condition of the horn.

In addition to good farriery, hoof condition can sometimes be improved in the long term by adding limestone flour and cod liver oil to the diet to ensure that calcium and vitamins A and D are present in sufficient levels to encourage and promote healthy horn growth. Specially prepared compounds containing biotin are also available.

In hot, dry conditions the hoof wall may dry out and crack – moisture can be added by standing the horse in water for approximately fifteen minutes twice a day or more. Again, the time factor has to be considered in a busy yard. There is a range of hose boots available that hold the hose in position on the leg, allowing you to get on with some work. When leaving the horse with his hooves immersed in water, precautions must be taken to prevent the heels from getting cracked and sore. Rub petroleum jelly into the heels beforehand and dry the heels carefully afterward.

After soaking the hoof walls thoroughly, rub in a moisturising product to help seal in the absorbed water.

In extremely wet conditions the hoof walls will soften, which may cause foot soreness in the unshod horse. In a shod horse, shoes may become loose as the horn softens. In such conditions, try to bring the horse in from the fields regularly to allow the hooves to dry out.

Shoeing
The Normal Functions of the Foot

When discussing shoeing, the normal functions of the foot must be considered. Shoeing must not adversely affect the foot's ability to perform these functions. The functions of the foot are:

- To bear the horse's weight.
- To reduce concussion and promote blood circulation.
- To protect sensitive internal structures.
- To act as a defence aid when used for kicking and striking out.

As the foot touches the ground, weight is transmitted via the bones to the bearing surfaces of the hoof and **frog**. Because the heel comes to the ground first, the important anti-concussion structures are at the rear of the foot.

Pressure on the frog exerts pressure onto the **digital cushion** which forces the **lateral cartilages** apart, against the horny wall. This flattens and empties the blood vessels between the lateral cartilages and the wall. At this stage the heels expand approximately 1.8–2.5 mm (0.08 in), depending upon the size of the horse.

Once the pressure is relieved when the foot is lifted off the ground, the foot will contract slightly, relaxing the digital cushion, so the blood vessels between the lateral cartilages and the wall will refill.

Factors which affect the correct functioning of the foot include:

- The nature of the going underfoot. A compressible material such as earth or sand will pack into the hoof, which helps exert pressure on the frog and promotes correct hoof function. As the surface compresses, concussion is greatly reduced. Working for long periods on a surface such as tarmac causes increased concussion and, if the frog is not contacting the ground, a reduction in circulatory efficiency within the foot.

- The size of the foot in relation to the size of the horse. If the hooves are very small in relation to the size of the horse they will be less efficient at absorbing concussion. Over-large feet don't tend to cause as much of a problem, other than that the horse may be a bit clumsy and/or flat-footed.

- Any defective conformation of the foot, e.g. a boxy foot, will not have such an effective anti-concussion mechanism as the frog doesn't normally make contact with the ground. This will also affect the efficiency of the circulation within the foot.

- Incorrect shoeing, for example, heels too short therefore not allowing for expansion of the foot as it comes into contact with the ground. Nailing too far back and too tightly at the heel will have the same detrimental effect.

Why Horses Need Shoeing

Reasons for shoeing include:

- It enables the horse to work both on and off the roads without excessive wear to the feet, which helps prevent footsoreness.
- It prevents the horny hoof wall from being worn out faster than the rate of growth.
- It improves grip on grass and allows the use of studs for competition purposes.
- It helps reduce the softening effects of excessive wet and moisture.
- It may help to correct defects or ailments of the foot.

As a rough guide, the horse will need to be re-shod every five to seven weeks. If the horse is in very hard work or is prone to losing shoes he will need to be shod more frequently. The reason why he is losing shoes must also be determined. Youngsters are often fitted with front shoes only to begin with – as their workload increases, hind shoes can be added. It is possible to keep some horses unshod if they are not working particularly hard or are just hacking out on suitable going. However, they will still need to have their feet trimmed regularly to ensure even development and balance of the hoof wall. Most small ponies can work unshod as they tend to have good quality horn and tough hooves.

Signs that the Horse Needs Re-shoeing

- Between five and seven weeks have elapsed since the farrier last attended to the horse.
- A shoe is loose or has slipped inwards.
- The shoe is excessively worn.
- The **clenches** have risen.
- A shoe has been cast (lost).
- The foot has grown long and out of shape.
- The wall overhangs the shoe.
- The hoof wall has cracked and split badly. This will reduce the security of the shoe.

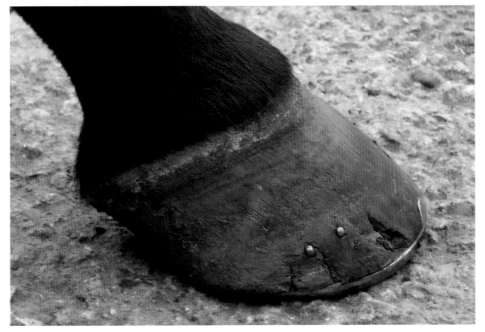

Figure 7 A foot in need of re-shoeing

ITQ 32 Give three reasons why horses are shod.

ITQ 33 What can be added to the diet to help improve hoof condition?

ITQ 34 What problems can affect the hoof wall in:
a. Very dry conditions?

b. Very wet conditions?

Preparation for the Farrier's Visit

Always book appointments with the farrier well in advance. Leaving it until the last minute means you may have a long wait, resulting in a lost shoe or other problems.

Ensure that the horse is well used to being handled and having his feet lifted and picked out. Someone competent must be on hand to meet the farrier and available to assist if necessary. The horse must be ready – stabled with clean, dry legs – and there must be a secure ring and weak link to which the horse can be tied.

If possible, provide a level and clean surface for the farrier to work on, preferably with a non-slip floor. In winter, a well-lit, sheltered area is desirable.

Handling the Unruly Horse

Although some horses are nervous by nature, few are aggressive. If a horse is well handled from birth and taught to stand while having his feet attended to, there should be no problems when the farrier visits. However, if a horse is difficult, it must be agreed between the farrier and owner how the horse is to be restrained and/or reprimanded. The farrier will normally use his voice to correct the horse. If vocal reprimands are insufficient, further means of restraint such as a bridle or twitch will have to be used. In severe cases it may be necessary, after consultation with the vet, to use some form of sedative.

Methods of Shoeing

Shoeing may be carried out either hot or cold. Hot shoeing is the process whereby the shoes are made red-hot in a forge and then fitted and shaped whilst hot. A forge is needed for hot shoeing. Most farriers have a portable forge and will come out to you. If your farrier doesn't have a portable forge, you will have to take your horse to the farrier's premises.

A forge is not needed for cold shoeing – the process is the same as for hot, but the shoes are fitted cold. For cold shoeing, it is especially important that farrier knows the size and pattern of shoe that fits your horse.

The Hot Shoeing Process

1. Removal. The first stage involves removing the old shoes. This is done by first knocking up the clenches (folded over nails) with the **buffer** and **driving hammer**. The flat end of the buffer is placed under the clench and, when struck by the hammer, prises the clench up. When all the clenches have been knocked up, the shoe is levered off with the **pincers**. The pincers are used starting at the heels, working towards the toe with a downward-pulling action.

The farrier supports the front foot and lower limb by holding it between his legs. This keeps his hands free. The hind leg is supported on the farrier's thigh.

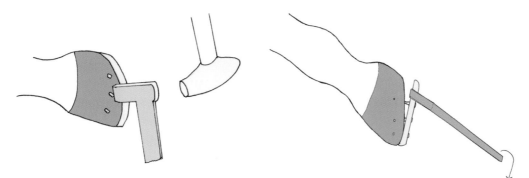

The buffer is used to knock up the clenches

The pincers prise the shoe off, working from the heels downward

Figure 8 Removing the shoe

2. Preparation. The excess horn is cut away with either **hoof cutters** or a **drawing knife**. Ragged bits of the frog are cut off. It is important that the frog is not cut excessively as it may then be unable to perform its functions properly. The **rasp** is used to give a level bearing surface upon which the shoe will rest. The drawing knife is used to make a notch in the wall for the toe clip to rest in.

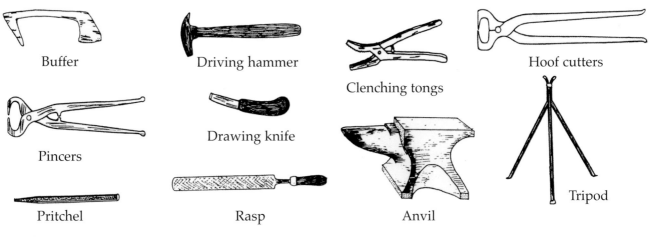

Buffer

Driving hammer

Clenching tongs

Hoof cutters

Pincers

Drawing knife

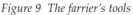

Pritchel

Rasp

Anvil

Tripod

Figure 9 The farrier's tools

ITQ 35 List five signs that the horse needs re-shoeing.

3. Forging. This is the process of making a new shoe, although many farriers buy in ready-made shoes. It is important that the correct weight of iron and size of shoe are used to suit each individual horse or pony. The shoe is put in the forge and made red-hot. It is then removed using the **fire tongs** and placed on the **anvil**. The farrier will use the **shoe tongs** to hold the shoe and the **turning hammer** to shape it as needed. He will then knock the **pritchel** into one of the nail holes so that he can carry the shoe to the horse.

If the shoe is made up from scratch, iron of the correct length and weight is cut. The iron is held in the forge until red-hot, then shaped around the anvil. The nail holes are stamped in and finally toe or quarter clips are drawn. (The front shoes have toe clips and the hind shoes have quarter clips to help hold the shoe in place.) Toe clips are not used behind as this would exacerbate overreaching (the toe of the hind foot striking the heel of the front foot, causing bruising or laceration). The toe of the hind shoe may be rounded off (rolled) to reduce any damage done in the event of the horse overreaching.

4. Fitting. Whilst the shoe is red-hot, it is fitted onto the foot. This burns the horn and gives the farrier an indication as to what alterations are necessary. The horse cannot feel the shoe being fitted as the outer horn is insensitive. The shoe is once again held on the anvil and hammered until it is exactly the right shape for the horse's foot.

5. Nailing on. When the farrier is happy with the fit of the shoe it is immersed in cold water to cool it down (quenched). Shoeing nails are used to hold the shoe in place. Nailing is a very skilled job as the nails must never press on or puncture the sensitive **laminae**. A mistake made whilst nailing on could make a horse lame.

Shoeing nails vary in size and are bevelled on one side. The nails are driven in with the bevel to the inside to send the nail outwards, thus reducing the risk of the nail penetrating the sensitive foot. As each nail is driven in the point is twisted off, leaving just enough to make a clench. The nails are never sent back in the old nail holes, but always go in a slightly different position to ensure a good hold.

Seven nails are normally used: three on the inner edge of the shoe and four on the outer edge.

6. Finishing off. When nailing on of a shoe is complete the horse stands with his leg drawn forwards and his foot on a metal **tripod**. The rasp is used to make a bed for the clenches, which are then either hammered down neatly until level with the wall of the hoof, or pulled down tightly with the **clenching tongs**.

The clenches should be the correct distance up the hoof wall – approximately a third of the way up – and appear fairly level. If the clenches are too low the shoe may be wrenched off easily. This is known as **fine nailing**. **Coarse nailing** is when the clenches are too high up the wall. In this case, there is a danger of the nails pressing on the sensitive laminae within the foot.

The clips of the shoe are embedded into shallow grooves to help prevent the shoes from slipping and the rasp is lightly run around the foot where it meets the shoe to ensure a neat finish.

Removes or Refits

If a horse has not been out on the road very much, his shoes may not be very worn. In this case the shoes may be removed, the feet trimmed and prepared and the old shoes put back on. This process is called fitting **removes**.

ITQ 36 Name the tools used by the farrier and describe how a shoe is removed.

Points to look for in a well-shod foot

To assess whether a horse has been well shod, look for the following points:

1. The horse must be completely sound and able to move freely and comfortably.

2. The foot must be in balance, i.e. of a shape that provides even support to the horse's weight and permits optimum movement.

3. The shoe must be made to fit the foot and not vice versa. If the toe has been cut back too much it is known as **dumping** and can adversely affect the balance of the foot.

4. The foot must be evenly reduced in size at the toe and heel, inside and outside of the foot.

5. The correct type of shoe and weight of iron must be used according to the size of the horse and the work he is required to do. A small pony would have a lighter iron than a large hunter.

6. The rasp must not be used excessively on the hoof wall as this would remove the protective **periople**, which may lead to drying out of the wall.

7. There should not be excessive use of the knife on the sole or frog. The frog should ideally be in contact with the ground – it cannot perform its functions if it does not touch the ground.

8. The correct number of nails has been used. There are normally seven, three on the inside and four on the outside. However, this may vary, with fewer nails being used if the hoof is of poor quality.

9. The correct size of nail must be used. The nail head should be neither too large nor too small and should fit the nail holes in the shoe so that they are level with the surface of the shoe.

10. The nail holes must be evenly spaced between the toe and the quarter.

11. The clenches must be even and approximately one third of the way up the wall.

12. No daylight must show between the foot and the shoe.

13. The groove for the toes and quarter clips must be neat. The clips must be neatly embedded in.

14. The heels must not be too short or too long.

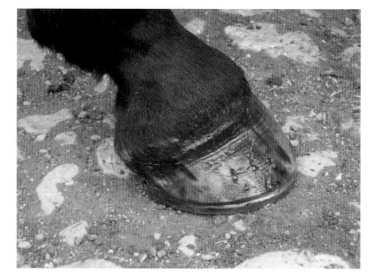

Figure 10 A well-shod foot

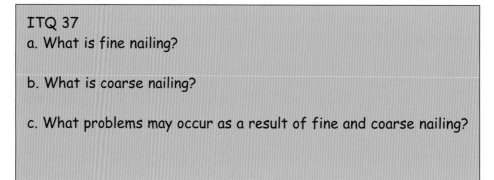

ITQ 37
a. What is fine nailing?

b. What is coarse nailing?

c. What problems may occur as a result of fine and coarse nailing?

ITQ 38 List four important factors that indicate a well-shod foot.

ITQ 39 Why should the rasp not be used excessively on the hoof wall?

ITQ 40 Once shod, why is it important that the horse's heels can expand?

Studs

There are occasions when extra grip is needed when riding, e.g. when competing in wet and/or slippery conditions. Most competition horses are fitted with studs at shows and events. If studs are required, the farrier will drill one stud hole into the outer heel of each shoe before fitting. Horses competing at the higher levels may have a stud hole in both heels of the shoe and wear two studs in each shoe.

In between shows, stud holes should be kept clean, packed with a small piece of oily cotton wool, otherwise they will become clogged with dirt and corroded, to the extent that it will be difficult or impossible to fit the studs. The studs, too, must be kept dry, ideally wrapped in an oily cloth to stop them from rusting. In the stud kit you must keep a narrow ended tool (or a nail) to loosen dirt and cotton wool out of the stud holes, a **stud tap**, used to clean the stud holes and thread, and a small spanner, used to tighten the studs into position.

Before you begin to use studs, it is sensible to ask the advice of an experienced horseman or the farrier, as there are many different types of stud available. For jumping, large pointed or square studs are used. These must never be worn when riding on the road, as they will unbalance the feet and cause uneven strain on the legs. Small, flat **road studs** may be used if hacking out in slippery conditions. As an alternative to road studs, **stud nails** (sometimes called road nails) can be used. They have a toughened nail head which provides extra grip when hacking on the road. If the horse is prone to slipping, ask the farrier to use one or two stud nails in each shoe. (Note that, unlike threaded studs, stud nails are permanent fixtures for the life of the shoe.)

Figure 11 Studs

IN-TEXT ACTIVITY

a. Find out about three topical products that claim to promote healthy horn growth.

b. List their active compounds and explain why they are supposed to improve hoof condition.

c. Find out about three dietary supplements formulated to improve hoof condition.

d. List their active compounds and explain the function/s of each.

ITQ 41 What are the anti-concussion mechanisms within the foot?

WORMING

We now look at another of the most important aspects of prophylactic management – worming. Failure to control worm infestations can have dangerous and sometimes fatal results.

All horses harbour worms (also called **internal parasites**), which can cause irreparable damage to their internal systems. The level of infestation must be controlled by the regular use of an effective drug (an **anthelmintic**). The frequency with which horses must be wormed is dependant on the type of drug and time of year.

Ways in which Internal Parasites Affect Health

- Primary damage to the gut linings, which impairs the absorption of nutrients.

- Secondary damage to the gut linings by stopping or reducing blood flow, causing death of the tissue (**necrosis**). Food cannot pass normally through the dead section, which results in colic.

- The larval forms of some worms travel through the walls of the intestine, enter the small arterioles then migrate through the arteries, moving against the flow of blood. Some travel to the heart, causing valve damage, inflammation, and weakening. The damage will never be corrected and may lead to death eventually. Furthermore, death occurring as a result of damage to the heart and surrounding blood vessels may be sudden, quite possibly while the horse is being ridden, putting the unsuspecting rider in jeopardy.

- The adult worms cause anaemia by sucking blood. Ulceration, colic and diarrhoea may also occur.

Signs of Heavy Worm Infestation

- Dull and staring coat.
- General lack of condition, weight loss and depression.
- Anaemia – mucous membranes will be too pale (test for dehydration – see page 153).
- Diarrhoea and colic.
- Distended stomach.
- Loss of appetite.

Note: Even a horse who looks perfectly well and healthy will be harbouring some adult worms and eggs, and will still need to be wormed.

Life Cycles and Control of Main Types of Parasites

Let's look more specifically at the life cycles of the main types of worm.

Large Strongyles

Also known as the **redworm,** there are fifty species of large and small strongyle. The most common species to affect horses include:

Strongylus vulgaris   *Strongylus edentatus*
Strongylus equinus   *Tridontophorus*

The large strongyle is a reddish brown worm, 2–5 cm (approximately 1–2 in) long, and was once the most prevalent of the internal parasites affecting horses. Although the problem has been reduced by effective use of wormers, it is still a common cause of spasmodic colic.

Life cycle

1. The female worm attaches to the gut wall and sucks blood. She lays her eggs, which are passed out in the dung onto the pasture.

2. The eggs hatch into **first stage larvae** in as little as three days. The larvae feed on bacteria and become **second stage larvae**. In the final stage they become **infective larvae**, which wait on the grass stalks and are ingested either by a new host – another horse – or by the same horse, thereby causing re-infestation.

3. Once ingested, the larvae burrow into the intestinal wall and travel to the small arterioles of the blood supply. Migration along the arteries then occurs. Note that not every worming drug is effective against these migrating larvae (see Table 3, this chapter). Dependant upon the species, some larvae travel along the aorta, causing damage to heart valves; others enter the renal artery which supplies the kidneys. However, most of the larvae remain in the cranial mesenteric artery which supplies the intestines. Here they cause inflammation (**arteritis**), roughening of the arterial wall and **thrombosis** (clot formation). Clots may break off and cause blockages in the smaller arteries which supply the intestines. This reduces blood flow and impairs function, and can cause the affected section of the gut to become gangrenous, resulting in colic.

   The damaged arteries, wherever occurring, may be weakened and bulge. This is known as an **anuerism** which may collapse or burst, causing death. Large strongyle larvae cause many cases of colic.

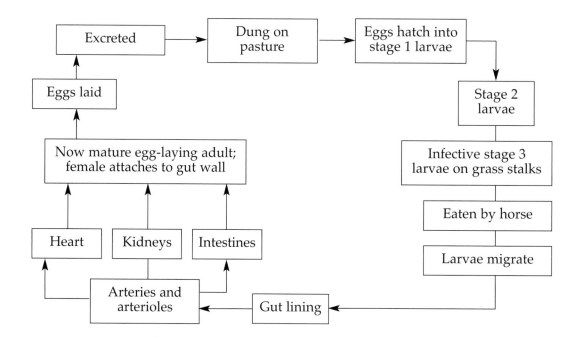

Figure 12 Life cycle of large strongyle

4. It takes between six and twelve months for the larvae of *Strongylus vulgaris* to mature into egg-laying adults, at which point they then return to the large intestine. The eggs are passed out in the dung.

ITQ 42 What damage is caused by migrating larvae?

Small Strongyle (Small Redworm) *Cyathostomus spp*

Also known as **cyathostomes,** small redworms – the adult worm range from 4–26 mm (usually less than an inch) in length – are a major cause of weight loss and diarrhoea in horses. The condition is termed **larval cyathostomosis** and the signs, usually seen between December and May, are:

- Gradual or rapid weight loss.
- Diarrhoea. This may accompany the weight loss, starting with the dung having a 'cowpat' appearance.
- Loss of performance – sluggish behaviour.
- Colic – this may be recurrent, with bouts lasting two to three days.
- Loss of appetite.
- Filled legs (and possibly abdomen and sheath in geldings).

Small redworm disease tends to affect horses under the age of six or from mid-teens onwards. It can affect horses that have been wormed regularly with routine doses.

Life cycle

The life cycle of these parasites takes between six and twelve weeks. In the summer months, the life cycle is very quick – the larvae develop into adults within a period of five weeks. In the autumn their development is prolonged and they remain as 3rd and 4th stage larvae as cysts within the gut wall. These are known as **encysted larvae**.

For reasons unknown, the larvae resume development in late winter or spring. Hundreds, possibly thousands of 4th stage larvae emerge from the cysts and cause irreparable damage, sometimes even death. Even before they emerge, large numbers of encysted larvae can cause serious illness.

In detail, the life cycle is as follows.

1. Eggs of the mature worm are passed out in the faeces. Within a week, infective stage 1 larvae develop, mature into stage 2 larvae and, as stage 3 larvae, are ingested by the horse.

2. The larvae migrate to the caecum and colon, where they penetrate the mucosal lining of the gut wall. The larvae are now termed 'encysted'. During the encysted phase, the development of the stage 3 larvae may be delayed, a phenomenon referred to as **inhibition**. Inhibition may last up to three years. Eventually they develop into stage 4 larvae.

3. There is a mass emergence of encysted larvae in late winter/early spring. The larvae may suck blood but most damage is caused by the effect of the burrowing into, and emergence from, the intestine walls.

4. The larvae then develop into egg-laying adults. The eggs are passed out in the faeces.

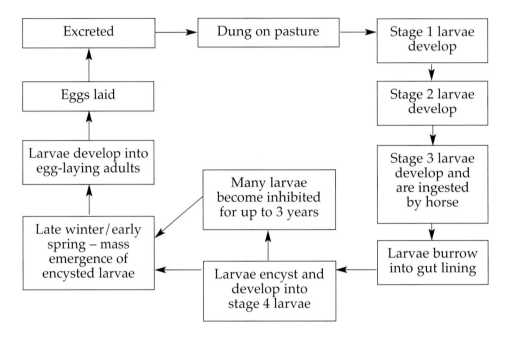

Figure 13 Life cycle of small strongyle

Prevention of small redworm disease

● Worm regularly every 4–6 weeks between March and September to remove egg-laying adults.

● Collect the dung from the pasture regularly.

● In early November, give Panacur Equine Guard for five consecutive days to remove the encysted larvae acquired during the summer months, this being the only wormer licensed to remove encysted redworm.

● Repeat this in February to remove larvae acquired during winter grazing.

ITQ 43 What are the signs of small redworm disease?

ITQ 44 How is damage caused by small redworm?

Ascarids (also called *Parascaris equorum*, Roundworm)

These heavily bodied worms measure up to 50 cm (20 in) in length and have a 10–12 week life cycle. Egg-laying adults can be found in the foal's small intestine at around twelve weeks old. Foals should therefore be wormed from six weeks of age – before the ascarids start laying eggs – with a wormer effective against ascarids – see Table 3 this chapter.) Between the age of eighteen months and two years, the horse develops immunity to ascarid infection.

Life cycle

1. The adult worm lays tough-coated adhesive eggs in the small intestine, which are then passed out in the faeces. The eggs stick to the surrounding area (including stable walls, floors etc.) and are very resistant to drying out. They can persist for many years.

2. On pasture, the larvae develop within six weeks. Once ingested they hatch and penetrate the wall of the intestine and are carried by the circulatory system to the heart, liver and other organs.

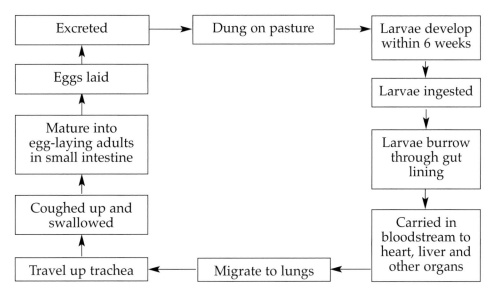

Figure 14 Life cycle of ascarid

3. Eventually they migrate to the lungs, break through the blood vessels into the lungs and travel up the trachea to be coughed up and swallowed.

4. Once swallowed they mature in the small intestine into egg-laying adults.

Tapeworm (*Anoplocephala perfoliata*, *Anoplocephala magna* and *Anoplocephaloides mamillana*)

Tapeworms are significant and potentially very damaging internal parasites. The mature adult measures up from 8–25 cm (3–10 in) in length, 8–14 mm ($^1/_3$ – $^1/_2$ in) in width and attaches to the gut wall by four suckers.

Adult tapeworms are normally found in large numbers at the junction of the small and large intestine, the **ileocaecal junction**, and are responsible for causing many cases of colic which require surgery (known as **surgical colics**). The incidence of tapeworm infection is high in areas which favour the intermediate host (areas with acidic soils, such as heathland).

It isn't always possible to determine the presence of tapeworms from a faecal examination as the techniques developed for showing roundworm infestations are not suitable.

Life cycle

1. Mature tapeworms shed segments which are passed in the dung. Occasionally the whole worm is passed. The segments break down, releasing eggs into the pasture.

2. The eggs are eaten by the **oribatid mite**, also called the **forage mite**, which acts as an intermediate host. The mite lives in the root mat – particularly on permanent pasture on acidic land – and is ingested by the grazing horse. The forage mite can also live in hay and straw. Within the forage mite, the eggs develop into larval tapeworms known as **cysticeroids**. This takes approximately four months.

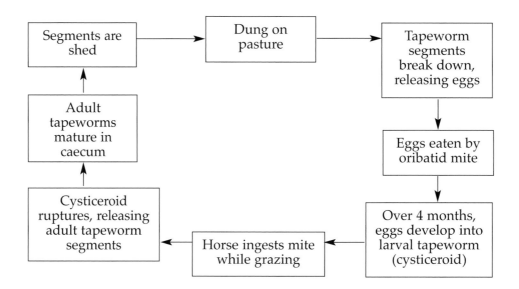

Figure 15 Life cycle of tapeworm

3. After a period of approximately eight weeks, the cysticeroid breaks out and ruptures, releasing adult tapeworm segments which then mature in the horse's caecum. Heavy infestations cause ulceration and blockages of the ileocaecal junction.

Control of tapeworm infestation

● Use a double dose of a pyrantel embonate wormer at six-monthly intervals (preferably in September and March)

> ITQ 45 Why is it important that tapeworm infestation is controlled?

ITQ 46 How is tapeworm infestation controlled?

Bots (*Gastrophilus spp*)

Although parasitic, bots are not worms – they are the larvae of the bot fly. The adult bot fly is about 1.25 cm (¹/₂ in) long and looks similar to a bee.

Life cycle

1. The female fly is active in the early summer and September and lays her eggs on the horse's coat, from where they are licked off by the horse.

2. From the horse's mouth, they burrow into the mucous membranes of the mouth, tongue and gums. In these warm, moist conditions the eggs develop into larvae and after a month migrate to the stomach lining. The mature larvae are reddish brown, approximately 2 cm (³/₄ in) long, with a broad, rounded body tapering to a narrow, hooked anterior.

3. In their development period of eight to ten months (over the winter months), the larvae attach themselves to the stomach lining which causes haemorrhaging, ulceration or perforation of the stomach. If not controlled this can lead to fatal peritonitis and intestinal blockage. These conditions may occur in the absence of noticeable signs.

4. In the spring, the larvae release their hold and are passed out in the faeces, then burrow into the ground and pupate. With three to ten weeks the adult fly emerges and the life cycle continues.

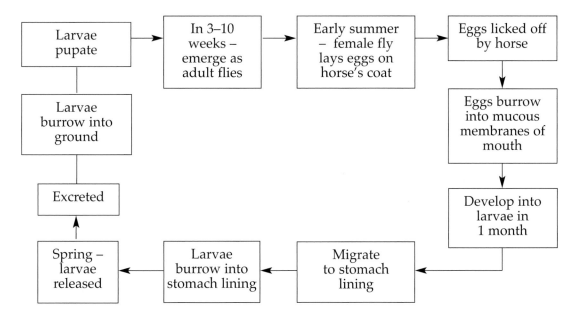

Figure 16 Life cycle of bot

To control bot infestation

● Worm the horse using ivermectin in December. By this time the frosts have killed the flies and the bot larvae have reached the stomach.

General Control of Parasite Infestation

This aspect of horse care may be divided into two areas – paddock management and chemical control, using drugs (anthelmintics), fly repellents and insecticides.

Paddock Management

This, whilst time-consuming, is quite straightforward and very important.

● Grazing should be kept clean through regular picking up of droppings (at least twice a week in the summer, once a week in a cold winter or twice a week in a mild winter).

● Over-grazing should be avoided, both by adhering to appropriate stocking levels and by periods of resting, which allow it to recover and regenerate.

● Long grass should be topped periodically.

● Graze with sheep or cattle. Once ingested, larvae will not develop into adult worms in sheep or cattle.

Chemical Control

There are a number of factors to be borne in mind if this is to be safe and effective.

● All new horses whose worming history is unknown must be wormed on arrival at the yard using an 'all in one' wormer, i.e. one containing ivermectin, which controls roundworm and bots, and praziquantel, which controls tapeworm. In winter, a five-day course of Panacur Equine Guard should be given.

● Broodmares must be treated every six weeks, *but note that some drugs are not suitable for pregnant mares* (see Table 3 this chapter, or check with your vet). It is particularly important that the pasture that broodmares and youngstock are turned out on is clean.

● Between the ages of four and six weeks, foals must be wormed and then treated every four weeks until eight months old, being sure to use the appropriate dosage. From that age onward, horses must be on a regular worming programme for the rest of their life.

● Weanlings are particularly at risk from small redworm disease at the end of a hot, dry summer. They should be dosed with Panacur Equine Guard in mid-October and then be turned out on clean pasture that has not been grazed by horses for at least five months.

- Groups of horses at grass together must be wormed at the same time.

- The stabled horse must be wormed regularly because he would have picked up worm larvae during any spell at grass. Therefore he may still have a worm burden and be suffering damage due to migrating larvae.

The interval between worming depends on various factors:

- **The type of drug.** Ivermectin compounds should be used every eight to ten weeks. Moxidectin should be administered every thirteen weeks; pyrantel compounds need to be used every four to eight weeks (see Table 3 for details).

- **The age of the horse.** Following manufacturers' instructions, weanlings and youngstock should be wormed more frequently than adult horses as the worm eggs reappear after a shorter period.

- **Stocking density.** Ideally there should not be more than one horse per acre. If there are more, the rate at which horses become infested increases, but more frequent worming should not be seen as a substitute for pasture management.

Horses sharing grazing should be wormed at the same time.

Administering Wormers

The amount of wormer needed depends upon the horse's bodyweight. Each manufacturer supplies information on dosage and this should be referred to.

Powders and pellets can be mixed in with the normal feed. If you have a sensitive, fussy feeder, add a delicacy that you know he is fond of, such as molasses, carrots or apples. Powders tend to be less expensive than pastes.

Pastes administered orally through a plastic syringe are fairly convenient to use provided you have a cooperative horse. Adjust the ring on the plunger shaft to give the correct dosage and squirt onto the back of the tongue. Then try to keep the horse's head up and mouth closed to stop him spitting out the wormer. (If he does manage to do this, he will need to be given more.) When wormer is being administered by syringe, the horse should be wearing a headcollar, but should not be tied up.

If your horse is not happy about taking paste from the syringe, squirt it into his feed or disguise it amongst some bread or titbits and either give by hand or mixed in with the feed.

Administration by stomach tube has to be done by the vet and is usually carried out only when a very large dose of wormer needs to be administered.

ITQ 47 When should a foal first be wormed?

ITQ 48 What can be done to reduce the risk of small redworm disease in weanlings?

Characteristics of Wormers

Wormers, which are marketed under several different brand names, have a number of different drugs as their active constituent, and thus are effective or ineffective against different types of parasite. In some circumstances, it is necessary to administer them in other than standard dosage to achieve certain results; in other cases, treatment may be more effective at certain times of year, because of the life cycle of the parasite being targeted. Some wormers are contra-indicated for youngstock, pregnant mares, etc. and, in some cases (discussed shortly) resistance to a particular drug may be built up by repeated use.

Table 3 gives a brief analysis of the characteristics of most of the drugs commonly available in the UK; where further information is required, or uncertainty exists, the manufacturer's literature or your own vet should be consulted.

Drug	Marketed as	Notes
Group 1		
Pyrantel embonate	Strongid-P Pyratape P	Double dosage needed to treat tapeworms in March and September. Pyrantel is the only drug effective against tapeworm. Not effective against worm eggs, encysted small redworm larvae, migrating large redworm larvae or bots.
Group 2		
Ivermectin	Eqvalan Equimax Eraquell Furexel Panomec	A very effective drug, active against the parasites mentioned in this chapter and migrating larvae at normal doses. It is effective against bots and should be administered in December when the frosts have killed the flies and the bot larvae have reached the stomach. Ivermectin is not licensed for the treatment of mucosal cyathostome (small redworm) larvae and is not effective against worm eggs or tapeworm.

Moxidectin	Equest	Moxidectin is released slowly into the horse's bloodstream so is effective for longer than other drug types. Broadly similar to ivermectin but this drug has shown activity against late encysted mucosal larvae of the small redworm. Effective against migrating large redworm and bots. Not effective against eggs, tapeworm or inhibited redworm larvae. *Not recommended for use in foals under the age of 4 months.* *Care must be taken not to overdose foals, small ponies and horses with low bodyweight.*
Group 3		
Fenbendazole	Panacur Panacur Equine Guard	Kills eggs, adults and larval stages of large and small strongyles. Panacur Equine Guard is the only product licensed to remove encysted small redworm.
Mebendazole Oxibendazole	Telmin Lincoln Horse and Pony Wormer	Have limited tapeworm control, do not control bots and resistance occurs in adult small redworm.
Group 4		
Praziquantel	Equimax	A new anthelmintic available in combination with ivermectin. Praziquantel is the only drug licensed to treat all three equine tapeworm species.

Table 3 Worming drugs

From the information given in Table 3, it is possible to devise an annual worming programme. That shown in Table 4 will provide a good degree of protection in most normal circumstances.

MONTH	DRUG
January	△
Middle of February	△ Panacur Equine Guard for five consecutive days to remove small redworm larvae acquired during winter grazing.
End of March	△ Double dose with pyrantel embonate to kill tapeworm.
April	△
Early May	△ Routine worming starts using ivermectin, moxidectin, pyrantel embonate or fenbendazole at recommended dosage and intervals.
June	△
July	△ Routine worming
August	△
September	△ After a heavy frost (which will kill forage mites), double dose with pyrantel embonate or give a routine dose of praziquantel to kill tapeworm.
October	△ ○
November	△ ○ Panacur Equine Guard for five consecutive days to remove encysted larvae acquired during summer.
December	△ ○ Ivermectin or moxidectin to remove bot larvae.

△   Treat every new horse with Panacur Equine Guard and then double dose with pyrantel on the 6th day.

○   Optimum time to treat migrating large redworm using fenbendazole, ivermectin or moxidectin.

Table 4 Worming programme

Resistance

If one particular type of drug is used continually for long periods (more than one year), certain worm species can begin to demonstrate resistance. Then, as they are not controlled by the routine worming programme, they quickly become dominant in the worm population.

Although this may potentially occur across a range of species and products, the most recent example of this is within the cyathostome family – adult small redworms have developed resistance to the **benzimidazole** group of wormers. This group includes the drugs mebendazole, fenbendazole and oxibendazole.

It should be noted from this that worms resistant to one particular drug will usually show **cross-resistance**; that is resistance to other wormers from the same chemical group. Therefore, when alternating brands of wormer, it is necessary to check on the active drug in order to minimize the risk of cross-resistance. In terms of routine worming, the chemical group should be changed once a year *not every time the horse is wormed.*

ITQ 49 How often should adult horses be wormed:

a. With ivermectin compounds?   Every ....weeks.

b. With pyrantel compounds?   Every .... weeks.

c. With moxidectin compounds?   Every .... weeks.

ITQ 50

a. When is the optimum time to treat bots?

b. What drug should be used?

ITQ 51 List three steps that can help prevent and control small redworm disease.

ITQ 52

a. What is meant by 'cross-resistance'?

b. How often should the drug used for routine worming be changed?

DENTAL CARE

The horse's molars should be inspected for sharp edges every six months. Sharp edges need to be rasped down by a vet or equine dentist approximately once a year, although this is variable and some horses may need more frequent attention.

The cheek teeth of the upper jaw are set wider apart than those in the lower jaw. The circular grinding action when the horse chews causes the inside edges of the lower molars and the outside edges of the upper molars to become sharp, sometimes with hooks developing.

A horse with sharp teeth will not be able to chew his food properly, which may cause food to fall out of his mouth (quidding) or cause the food to pass partly undigested through his system. In extreme cases it may deter the horse from even trying to eat his food, which will lead to hunger and loss of condition. Also, ulcers can develop on the inside of the cheeks and on the edge of the tongue, which will prevent the horse from eating properly and cause discomfort when he is working.

As horses get older the teeth may become loose making it difficult to chew properly. In older horses, look out for quidding and loss of condition.

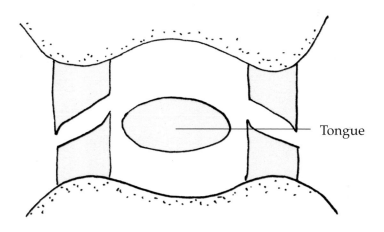

Figure 17 Molars, showing sharp edges

To check the teeth for sharp edges:
- The horse should wear a headcollar but not be tied up in case he pulls back.
- Gently but firmly take hold of the horse's tongue and bring it out to the side of the mouth, in the space between the teeth (the inter-dental space). Don't hold the tongue over the lower molars as you do this because, if the edges are sharp, the tongue can be cut.
- Use your free hand to quickly feel the outer edges of the upper molars.
- Repeat this on the other side of the mouth.
- The inner edges of the lower teeth shouldn't be felt in this way as you could be bitten. Try to inspect these visually. A small torch is useful when inspecting the back molars.

Some horses object to this procedure and may need to be restrained or sedated so that the vet or dentist can make a full assessment of the teeth and rasp them properly. In fact, it is preferable and safer to leave the procedure to the vet or dentist as they use a specially designed gag to keep the horse's mouth open.

VACCINATIONS

In the UK horses are most commonly vaccinated against tetanus, equine influenza and equine herpes virus (EHV).

Tetanus, also known as **lockjaw**, is a fatal disease caused when the tetanus bacteria *Clostridium tetani* invade the body through an open wound. All horses should be vaccinated against tetanus.

If a pregnant mare is vaccinated in the last month of pregnancy the foal will be protected for the first three months of his life. After that he will need to be vaccinated.

Anti-tetanus vaccinations should be given every two to five years unless otherwise advised by the vet, e.g. in areas of high tetanus incidence.

Equine influenza is a highly infectious disease caused by different strains of virus. It is necessary to vaccinate every ten to eleven months. Documentary proof of up-to-date vaccination against equine influenza is a requirement of entry into some forms of competition, and some showgrounds.

Tetanus and influenza vaccinations are normally available in combination if both are needed.

Equine herpes virus (EHV) causes respiratory disease, abortion, neonatal deaths and/or paralytic disease and 75 per cent of horses become latent carriers. The respiratory form is widespread in foals and yearlings. Youngstock who have been repeatedly infected in the first two years of life will 'shed' the virus: for this reason youngstock should be kept away from pregnant mares. Unvaccinated maiden or broodmares can also infect the pregnant mares. Breeding stock are most commonly vaccinated against EHV.

It is possible to vaccinate against EHV and equine influenza in one vaccination. The type of vaccine used will determine when and how frequently the horse will need to be vaccinated.

CHAPTER SUMMARY

This chapter has introduced the principles of routine health care, of which daily management is an integral part. It is helpful to use the 'five freedoms' as a gauge when managing horses – by assessing their daily management against the criteria of these freedoms and taking appropriate action combined with good 'preventative' management, the horse's psychological and physiological needs should be met.

CHAPTER 3

NUTRIENTS FOR HEALTH

The aims and objectives of this chapter are to explain:

- Why the horse needs a balanced diet.
- Which nutrients are needed by the horse.
- The functions of the different nutrients.
- The sources of the different nutrients.

The need for a balanced diet can be summarized in simple terms. Such a diet is essential in order to:

1. Sustain life and maintain health.
2. Provide energy for basic daily activity and maintenance of condition.
3. Provide energy for increased work.
4. Provide warmth.
5. Provide the nutrients necessary for all body processes including healthy growth.
6. Satisfy the appetite and the psychological need to chew.

If these criteria are to be met, each horse's diet must contain the correct balance of nutrients for his individual requirements at any given time. The various feedstuffs contain different levels of particular nutrients, each of which plays a vital role in the horse's well-being. Therefore, we need to understand what these nutrients are, what contribution they make to the horse's metabolism and where they can be sourced.

CLASSIFYING NUTRIENTS

Nutrients can be broadly divided into the following categories.

Carbohydrates are the main energy source. Energy is needed for all bodily functions including breathing, eating, moving, growing, pregnancy and lactation.

Lipids (fats and oils) provide an additional source of energy and provide essential fatty acids that the horse cannot synthesize.

Proteins provide a source of **amino acids** that are essential for growth, repair and renewal of body tissues, health during pregnancy and lactation.

Water constitutes approximately 70 per cent of the horse's bodyweight. As with all animals, water plays a vital part in the construction and functions of the horse's body.

Vitamins and minerals are essential for many body functions. Deficiencies may show as clinical signs ranging from cracked hooves to infertility.

These nutrients are further classified as **macro-nutrients** or **micro-nutrients** according to the quantities in which they are needed. As the names suggest, macro-nutrients are needed in larger quantities than micro-nutrients but that does not mean the latter are unimportant. We will now look at both categories in greater detail.

MACRO-NUTRIENTS
Carbohydrates
Carbohydrates are chemical substances made up of carbon, hydrogen and oxygen, found in plant and animal cells. Their functions are to store and yield energy. They are initially formed by plants as a result of **photosynthesis**, the process whereby the plant harnesses the energy of the sun to convert carbon dioxide and water into a food source, which is then stored within the plant's tissue as **soluble** and **insoluble carbohydrates**. Soluble carbohydrates include **sugars** and **fructan** and insoluble carbohydrates include **starch** and the structural carbohydrate **cellulose**. When the plant material is eaten by the horse, **sugars** and **starch** are broken down primarily in the small intestine by chemical enzymes, whereas fructans and structural carbohydrates such as cellulose are fermented in the large intestine by resident micro-organisms.

In addition to being sourced and digested differently, sugars and starch have different nutritional roles.

Monosaccharides or single sugars are the building blocks of the more complex carbohydrates. The most common single sugar is **glucose**. Two single sugars may combine to form a **disaccharide** or double sugar, for example glucose and **fructose** combined form **sucrose**; this is particularly abundant in grass and unrefined sugar beet.

Glucose and **galactose** (another single sugar) combined form **lactose,** which is found in milk. Following digestion, glucose is absorbed into the bloodstream and either transported to the cells for use as an immediate energy supply or converted to a **polysaccharide, glycogen,** and stored in the liver or muscles. Polysaccharides are made up of long chains of sugar molecules, containing between a few hundred and several thousand units.

Starch is the storage carbohydrate found in many plants and is a polysaccharide. Starch grains are abundant in the part of a plant concerned with storage; for example tubers such as potatoes and swedes act as starch stores for their respective plants. Roots and tubers consist of approximately 30 per cent starch whilst cereal starch content may vary from 40 per cent in oats to 70 per cent in maize.

Cellulose is a structural carbohydrate in plants. All plant cell walls are strengthened by structural carbohydrates such as cellulose and **hemicellulose**. (As plants mature they also develop a further structural component called **lignin**, which is not strictly a carbohydrate. Lignin cannot be digested by the horse's gut and therefore passes out in the faeces undigested. Unfortunately, the presence of lignin in mature plants makes them less digestible.) In the wild, cellulose and other structural carbohydrates would provide the bulk of the horse's energy. They are fermented by micro-organisms in the large intestine, resulting in an end-product of **volatile fatty acids** (**VFA's**). The most common VFA's are **acetic, proprionic and butyric acids**. These are absorbed and used as an energy source.

As well as being a very important source of energy, structural carbohydrates provide the bulk or roughage which is also essential in every horse's diet to maintain normal digestion through its sheer volume in the digestive tract. The stabled horse's fibre requirements are met easily when hay is fed.

ITQ 53 Which of the carbohydrates are soluble?

ITQ 54 Which of the carbohydrates are insoluble?

ITQ 55

a. What is a polysaccharide?

b. Give one example of a polysaccharide.

Lipids (Fats and Oils)

Lipids are stored within the body as **triglycerides**, which are compounds of **glycerol** and **fatty acids** containing carbon, hydrogen and oxygen. Some fatty acids are essential (i.e. they must be provided by the diet as they cannot be synthesized) – deficiencies of **linoleic** and **linolenic acid** can lead to growth impairment, failure of the reproductive system and kidneys, and skin lesions, although these deficiencies have not been widely reported in equines.

Triglycerides are mainly stored as subcutaneous fat, but a certain amount is held in the muscles and other tissues. The store of fat beneath the skin prevents excessive heat loss as well as providing a source of energy when needed.

It should be noted that carbohydrates can be readily converted to, and stored as, fat when energy intake exceeds requirements. Although the horse uses fat in the form of fatty acids as a major energy source, the horse's diet is traditionally low in fats and oil, generally containing only about 4 per cent of these substances. This is in contrast to the high content of both structural and non-structural carbohydrates. Lipids in the form of oils do, however, yield twice as much energy per gram as carbohydrates. This source of energy is useful if one is trying to reduce the dependence upon non-structural carbohydrates (starch and sugar) as an energy source, for example to manage problems such as exertional rhabdomyolysis (azoturia) and laminitis, where too much starch and sugar may contribute to their onset.

Studies have shown that dietary fat, e.g. corn or vegetable oil, is readily digested and actually lessens the decline in blood glucose levels during exercise, thereby delaying the onset of fatigue and accelerating recovery. Feeding oil over a prolonged period results in an increase in the ability to use stores of body fat as an energy source during exercise and spares the use of muscle and liver glycogen. (Glycogen depletion is a major cause of fatigue in low- intensity endurance exercise.)

As a result, it is now becoming more common to use oils in the diet of both endurance and performance horses. Oil is also a more frequent addition to low-energy feeds as it allows a greater emphasis on fibre-based energy sources and allows starch levels to be reduced. Feeds containing high levels have been linked to exuberant behaviour in some horses.

Proteins

Proteins are complex organic compounds made up of combinations of building blocks or sub-units known as **amino acids**.

There are seven main classes of body proteins:

1. Structural – for example **keratin** (hair), **collagen** and **elastin** (tendons, ligaments).
2. Contractile – for example, concerned with muscle contraction.
3. Storage – for example **ovalbumin**, which supplies amino acids to the developing embryo.
4. Defence – antibodies.
5. Signal – hormones.
6. Transport – for example **haemoglobin** in the blood.
7. Enzymes – promote and regulate most chemical reactions in the body.

Twenty-three types of amino acid have been identified. Each is made up of a different combination of some or all of the following elements: nitrogen, carbon, hydrogen, sulphur, phosphorus, iron and oxygen – and no two proteins will have exactly the same combination of amino acids.

All but ten of the amino acids can be synthesized in the horse's body from the conversion of one amino acid to another. These amino acids are known as **non-essential** or **dispensable amino acids.** The other ten cannot be synthesized and must therefore be provided in the diet. They are known as **essential** or **indispensable amino acids.**

Essential Amino Acids
Histidine
Isoleucine
Leucine
Lysine
Methionine
Phenylalanine
Threonine
Tryptophan
Valine

Table 5 The essential amino acids

The quality of a protein source is determined by its digestibility and the proportion of essential amino acids present relative to its total protein content. Proteins containing a high proportion of the essential amino acids are said to be high quality protein sources with a **high biological value (HBV proteins)** while those containing a low proportion of essential amino acids are said to be low quality protein sources, having a **low biological value (LBV proteins)**.

Animal proteins such as those found in eggs and milk are of a high biological value, as are a few plant proteins such as those found in soya beans. The proteins in many cereals contain a relatively lower level of essential amino acids and are, therefore, of low biological value. However, as horses are fundamentally herbivores, HBV proteins for their nutrition should, where possible, be sourced from plant material.

Lysine and **threonine** are the two first limiting amino acids in the body. This means that protein can only be utilized in accordance with the levels of lysine and threonine in the body. Deficiencies of these amino acids will adversely affect protein synthesis, resulting in impaired growth, so it is essential that optimum levels are maintained. All cereals are known to be low in lysine, however soya bean meal is a very good source. Manufacturers of compound feeds supplement their products to ensure correct levels of lysine and threonine.

Amino acids are taken into the horse's system when, during digestion, enzymes secreted from the wall of the small intestine release them to be absorbed into the portal blood system and circulated throughout the body, to be used for growth and tissue repair. The circulating amino acids are known as the **amino acid pool**.

Excess amino acids are broken down (**deaminated**) in the liver and removed by the kidneys as urea. Some amino acids will also be stored as blood albumin.

A certain amount of energy can be derived from excess dietary protein and some amino acids, such as **alanine**, can be converted to glucose. This generally happens only in abnormal circumstances, such as starvation, when tissue protein is used as a source of energy.

Tissue proteins are also broken down to amino acids and resynthesized during normal daily maintenance. The demand for amino acids is regulated by each horse's physiological needs – a young growing horse needs more than an adult horse.

ITQ 56 What percentage of the horse's diet is normally made up of lipids?

ITQ 57 Name the compounds of which lipids are comprised.

ITQ 58 What is the difference between essential and non-essential amino acids?

ITQ 59 What is the main function of protein in the diet?

ITQ 60 List the seven main classes of body proteins.

ITQ 61
a. Name the two dietary limiting amino acids.

b. What happens to excess amino acids?

ITQ 62 What determines the quality of a protein?

Water

Approximately 70 per cent of the horse's bodyweight is composed of water. The exact percentage is dependent on age and condition. Of this percentage two-thirds is intracellular (within the cells), maintaining cell rigidity, while the other third is extracellular (in the plasma and digestive tract).

The functions of water within the body are:

1. It helps maintain body temperature by cooling through the loss of excess heat in sweat.

2. It gives shape to the body cells.

3. It acts as a solvent in which substances can be dissolved and as a means of conveyance from one part of the body to another.

4. It provides a medium in which chemical reactions occur.

5. It provides a base for urine, thus aiding the excretion of waste.

6. It provides the base of milk for lactating mares.

7. It aids digestion.

Factors affecting water intake:

1. Diet, for example whether the horse is at grass or eating dry concentrates and hay. A horse on pasture may drink less because of the moisture content of the grass.

2. Temperature and environment: horses drink more in hot, humid conditions.

3. Amount and type of work. Sweating will make a horse thirsty.

4. Access to salt and mineral blocks.

5. Health: a sick horse may be reluctant to drink.

As an approximate guide to the quantities of water required for maintenance, the normal daily requirement is 5 litres per 100 kg of bodyweight (approximately a gallon per 200 lb). A stabled large hunter would therefore drink about 37 litres (8 gallons) daily.

Clean, fresh water must be available to horse at all times. An exception to this would be just before fast speed work. However, never remove the water from a horse about to do a long-distance event, as dehydration is a serious problem. Free access to water at vet gates is essential to maintain hydration. A loss of 8 per cent of body water causes illness. Dehydration and heat stroke result from a loss of 15 per cent of body water.

For all regular supplies of water, change it frequently rather than just topping up, because water becomes stale as it absorbs ammonia from the atmosphere.

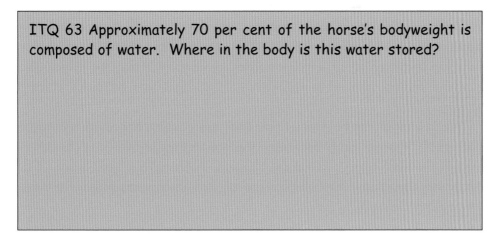

ITQ 63 Approximately 70 per cent of the horse's bodyweight is composed of water. Where in the body is this water stored?

MICRO-NUTRIENTS
Vitamins

Vitamins are organic compounds required in minute quantities, which ensure correct physiological function. The vitamin requirement varies with the level of exercise (stress leads to an increased requirement).

There are two categories of vitamins:

Fat-soluble vitamins, which may be stored in the liver. These include vitamins A, D, E and K.

Water-soluble vitamins, which may not be stored and include vitamin C andthe B complex.

We will look at these in further detail.

Fat-soluble Vitamins
Vitamin A (also known as **retinol**)
Functions:
– By boosting the horse's immune system, helps resistance to disease.
– Promotes healthy bone and tissue growth.
– May promote fertility.
– Improves night vision.

- Involved in metabolism of fats and carbohydrates.
- Linked to functioning of the thyroid gland, so is important in most body processes (e.g. development and growth).

Sources:
- Green leaves.
- Carrots.
- Good quality hay.
- Cod liver oil.

Food of plant origin does not contain pre-formed vitamin A but does contain vitamin A precursors called **carotenes**. The carotene present in green leaves is partially converted in the cells of the lining of the horse's small intestine into vitamin A, with the remainder being converted in the liver. Surplus vitamin A is stored in the liver. These stores may be exhausted over the winter as the horse can only store enough vitamin A to last approximately two months; this is when cod liver oil or another source of vitamin A may be given. The carotene content of feed is reduced by heat, light and oxidation during storage.

As this vitamin can be stored in the liver it is possible to provide excessive vitamin A. This can cause **toxicosis (hypervitaminosis)** which is character-ized by weight loss, bone decalcification, haemorrhage and poor coat. Chronic hypervitaminosis interferes with the function of other vitamins, especially vitamin D.

Deficiency signs:
- Suppressed appetite.
- Poor growth and loss of condition.
- Increased susceptibility to respiratory infections.
- Infertility.
- Skin disorders.
- Diarrhoea.

Vitamin D (also known as **calciferol** and 'the sunshine vitamin')
Functions:
Regulates the absorption of calcium and phosphorus in the body by affecting absorption in the gut, excretion by the kidneys and resorption from bone, thus preventing bone defects.

Sources:
- Made under the skin by the horse when in sunlight.
- Cod liver oil – necessary source in the winter.
- Sun-dried forages.
- Colostrum provides a rich source for the foal.

Deficiency signs:
- Swollen joints.
- Skeletal defects and lameness.

Excessive quantities can lead to ossification of soft tissue and high blood-calcium levels, which may lead to deposition in blood vessels, heart and joints.

Vitamin E (also known as **tocopherol** and the 'fertility vitamin')
Functions:
– Major function is as an antioxidant – i.e. it protects cell membranes from damage by oxidation by reducing the damaging effects of harmful substances called free radicals.
– Vitamin E works together with other antioxidants such as the selenium-containing enzyme **glutathione peroxidase**.
– Needed for normal muscular development and function.
– Thought to help in conditions such as exertional rhabdomyolysis (azoturia, tying up), but not actually proven yet.
– Supports normal immune system functions.

Sources:
– Fresh green forage.
– Grain.
– Alfalfa.
– Linseed oil.

Mares and stallions may benefit from additional vitamin E early on in the breeding season. High-performance horses need adequate supplies of vitamin E and may require a specific supplement of vitamin E and selenium, especially where dietary intake of oil is increased.

Deficiency signs:
– Poor performance.
– Adverse effects on immune function.
– Red blood cell defects.
– Degeneration of muscle tissue and, if combined with a selenium deficiency, liver damagemay occur.

Vitamin E deficiency may reduce reproductive performance in other species but evidence for this effect in horses has not been found.

Vitamin K (also known as **menaquinone**)
Function:
Aids the clotting of blood.

Sources:
– Bacteria synthesize the vitamin in the large intestine.
– Green food.

Deficiency signs:
Deficiency is rare, although any disruption in the normal balance of microflora in the hind gut (such as with certain antibiotics) may reduce the synthesis of vitamin K. some anticoagulant drugs will interfere with the effects of this vitamin.

Note: It is possible to overdose a horse with these fat-soluble vitamins as they can be stored. Also, an excess of one fat-soluble vitamin may reduce the absorption of another. Horses with impaired fat absorption may also see reduced absorption of the fat-soluble vitamins.

ITQ 64 What is hypervitaminosis?

ITQ 65
a. Give three functions of vitamin A.

b. State two sources of vitamin A.

ITQ 66
a. Give three functions of vitamin E.

b. State two sources of vitamin E.

Water-Soluble Vitamins

These cannot be stored in the body and excess vitamins are rapidly removed by the kidneys. Any disruption in the normal balance of microflora in the hind gut (such as induced by certain antibiotics) may reduce the rate of synthesis of these vitamins. Horses with a low-fibre diet may require additional supplementation.

The vitamin B complex

There are a number of vitamins within the B complex.

Vitamin B1 (also known as **thiamine**)
Functions:
This vitamin is involved in the production of energy – it regulates the metabolism of fats and carbohydrates, particularly glucose. It is also thought to have a 'quietening' effect as it is important for the health of the nervous system.

Sources:
– Synthesized by bacteria in the large intestine.
– Derived from most vegetables.

Deficiency signs:
– Impaired growth.
– Reduced appetite.
– Loss of condition.
– Incoordination.
– Nervousness.

Deficiency is rare unless bracken, which contains a B1 antagonist, is eaten.

Vitamin B2 (also known as **riboflavin)**
Functions:
– Aids the metabolism of proteins, carbohydrates and fats.
– Essential for normal growth.

Sources:
– Synthesized by bacteria in the large intestine.
– Grass.
– Dried yeast.

Deficiency signs:
– Reduced energy levels.
– Poor growth and condition.

Vitamin B6 (also known as **pyridoxine**)
Functions:
– Involved in the metabolism of fats, carbohydrates and proteins.
– Fifty enzymes are influenced by this vitamin.
– Involved in the production of haemoglobin.

Sources:
– Grass and green forages.

Deficiency signs:
Deficiency is not common in horses but would show as poor growth and changes to skin and blood.

Vitamin B3 (also known as **nicotinic acid** or **niacin**)
Functions:
– Promotes healthy skin.
– Involved in metabolic processes.
– Influences enzyme systems.

Sources:
– Synthesized from the amino acid tryptophan by bacteria in the large intestine.
– Cereals.

Deficiency signs:
Deficiency is not commonly seen in horses, but dermatitis would be likely to
be a sign.

Pantothenic acid
Functions:
– Involved in the metabolism of proteins, carbohydrates and fats.
– Involved in the formation of antibodies.

Source:
– Has to be supplied in the diet, from oats, barley, brewer's yeast, molasses.

Deficiency signs:
Deficiency is not common but would show as poor growth and condition.

ITQ 67 Give an alternative name for the following:
a. Retinol.

b. Calciferol.

c. Tocopherol.

d. Menaquinone.

ITQ 68
a. What is the function of vitamin B1?

b. What can cause deficiency of this vitamin?

Folic acid (also known as **folacin**)
Function:
Essential to the production of red blood cells

Sources:
– Grass.
– Green forage.
– Synthesized by bacteria in the large intestine.

Deficiency signs:
– Anaemia.
– Poor growth.
– Poor performance.

Biotin (also known as **Vitamin H**)

Functions:
- Aids metabolism of fat, protein and carbohydrates.
- Improves skin condition and hoof wall structure.
- Is associated with the sulphur-containing amino acid, methionine in relation to hoof horn quality.

Sources:
- Maize; biotin from most cereal sources is unavailable to the horse (the horse cannot utilize it).
- Yeast.
- Soya.
- Green forage.
- Biotin supplements (although not all biotin in supplements is available to the horse so they must be selected carefully).

Deficiency signs:
- Skin changes.
- Poor hoof condition.

Choline

Functions:
- Aids fat transportation in the body.
- Involved in nerve transmission (the neurotransmitter, **acetylcholine**).
- Is a component of cell membranes (forms part of **phospholipids**).

Sources:
- Oats, barley, sugar beet, linseed, molasses.

Deficiency signs:
Deficiencies are rare as it is widely found in feedstuffs and can be synthesized from the amino acid methionine.

Vitamin B12 (also known as **cobalamin**)

This vitamin contains the element cobalt.

Functions:
- Helps improve the appetite.
- Involved in the formation of red blood cells.
- Involved in the utilization of protein, therefore promotes growth.
- Aids reproductive processes.
- Aids the metabolism of carbohydrates, proteins and fats.
- In the presence of cobalt, bacteria synthesize B12 in the large intestine.

Sources:
- Oats, brewer's yeast.
- Synthetic vitamin supplement.

Deficiency signs:
- Anaemia, seen in youngsters more frequently than in mature horses.
- Poor growth.
- Infertility.
- Rough coat.

ITQ 69
a. What is the function of folic acid?

b. State three sources of folic acid.

ITQ 70 Give an alternative name for each of the following:
a. Thiamine.
b. Lactoflavin.
c. Vitamin B6.
d. Niacin.
e. Folacin.

ITQ 71 List the vitamins that the horse can synthesize within his body.

Vitamin C (also known as **ascorbic acid**)
Functions:
- Is an antioxidant.
- Involved in the formation of cartilage and bone.
- Aids the recovery from anaemia because it aids the utilization of iron (low vitamin C status has been associated with nosebleeds).
- Reduces stress.
- Improves skin problems.
- Fortifies the body's defence mechanism against disease.

Source:
Synthesized in the kidneys from dietary glucose.

Deficiency signs:
Since this vitamin is synthesized in the kidneys, deficiency doesn't usually occur in horses. However, it may be seen in post-operative horses, especially after colic surgery, or in very young animals. Supplementation may be warranted in old, ill or stressed animals.

Minerals

While all minerals are classed as micro-nutrients they may nevertheless be divided into two categories: **macro-minerals**, which are required in relatively large quantities and **trace minerals**, which are required in very small quantities. *Although essential in traces, if fed in abnormally high quantities, certain trace minerals prove toxic.*

All plants contain minerals; the types and quantities depend upon the type of plant and to what level the minerals are present in the soil. Some soils are mineral deficient; this will be reflected in the quality of any feedstuff grown.

Let us look at those minerals that are most essential to the horse.

Macro-Minerals

Calcium (Ca)

Functions:
- Important for healthy bone growth.
- Supports nerve and muscle function.
- Important for lactation.
- Aids blood coagulation.

Sources:
- Alfalfa.
- Grass and good hay.
- Sugar beet.
- Clover.
- Limestone flour.

Deficiency signs:
- If the deficiency is chronic, calcium is drawn from the skeleton, therefore weakening the bone.
- In older horses, bone decalcifies and fractures are more likely to occur.
- Skeletal defects, e.g. rickets and enlarged joints.
- Increased blood clotting time.
- Tying up (exertional rhabdomyolysis).

Phosphorus (P)

Functions:
- Promotes healthy bone growth.
- Involved in energy production.
- Involved in protein synthesis.

Sources:
- Good hay and grass.
- Cereals (high), especially bran.

Deficiency signs:
- Skeletal defects.
- Poor growth in youngsters.

Note: calcium and phosphorus can only be utilized when they are present in the correct ratio to each other and sufficient vitamin D is present.

It is essential for the horse's system to have a ratio of 2:1 calcium to phosphorus. If too much phosphorus is present in the diet it will inhibit the uptake and utilization of calcium and therefore lead to symptoms of calcium deficiency. Likewise excess calcium intake can be detrimental when severe.

Cereals, which are major constituents of many feeds, tend to have a higher quantity of phosphorus than calcium and thus have the potential to create an imbalance.

When dealing with young, growing horses, unless feeding a specially formulated coarse mix or cubes, it is essential that calcium is added to the diet in the form of limestone flour or alfalfa, for example. Vitamin D supplementation may also be required. Care must be taken when feeding bran because it is particularly high in phosphorus and so is not suitable for youngsters.

Almost all the calcium and 80 per cent of the phosphorus present in a horse is contained in the bones. During the final term of pregnancy and during lactation, calcium and phosphorus intake should be increased to prevent these minerals being drawn from the mare's skeleton and to ensure healthy growth of the developing foetus. The requirement for calcium and phosphorus in the lactating mare and in growing animals is of greater importance than the increased need for energy and so feeds should have a higher than usual percentage content of these minerals.

The correct balance of nutrients can be supplied to the pregnant and/or lactating mare by feeding a stud coarse mix or cubes or suitable balancer.

Sodium (Na)

Functions:
- Controls fluid balance within the body.
- Involved in transfer of nerve impulses.
- Needed for absorption of glucose and amino acids.
- Needed for normal muscle function.

Sources:
Most commonly sourced from common salt (sodium chloride) added to the feeds daily; may also be supplied in a salt and mineral block

Deficiency signs:
Along with potassium, sodium is lost in sweat. Although sweating is not, itself, a sign of deficiency, if a horse sweats a lot, this should be borne in mind when assessing dietary needs. Actual signs of deficiency are:
- Fatigue, particularly after strenuous exercise.
- Reduced feed and water consumption.
- Weight loss.
- Weakness.
- Dehydration.

Potassium (K)

Functions:
– Osmotic regulation of body fluids*.
– Control of acid / base balance (homeostasis)*.
– Nerve and muscle function.
– Metabolic uptake of carbohydrates.

Sources:
– All green plants.
– Hay.

Deficiency signs:
– Decreased growth rate.
– Suppressed appetite, similar to sodium deficiency.

Dietary excess is excreted in the urine. *Very high levels of potassium may interfere with the absorption of magnesium.*

Chlorine (Cl)

Functions:
– A component of bile salts and necessary in the gastric juices for the digestion of protein.
– Involved in body fluid regulation.
– Control of acid / base balance.

Sources:
Chlorine is a non-metallic element which, combined with sodium, makes the compound sodium chloride (common salt). It is also found in many supplements and compound feeds.

Deficiency signs:
Deficiency is unlikely, particularly when a mineral block is provided and / or concentrate cubes or coarse mix are fed. Where it occurs, it is most likely to be seen after heavy sweating, e.g. when working strenuously in hot, humid conditions. Signs are:
– Loss of appetite.
– Weight loss.
– Poor performance.

Magnesium (Mg)

Functions:
– Involved in the regulation of the calcium:phosphorus ratio.
– Aids the formation of bone and teeth.
– Involved in all forms of energy production.
– Involved in nerve and muscle function.
– Involved in cell metabolism.
– Activates over 300 enzymes.

*These process are explained in detail in Book 1 of this series – Anatomy and Physiology

Sources:

Most feedstuffs, in particular:

– Pulses.

– Linseed.

– Turnips.

– Carrots.

– Soya beans.

– Alfalfa.

– Good pasture.

– Well-made hay.

Approximately 65 per cent of body magnesium is found in the skeleton and teeth.

Deficiency signs:

– Nervous tension.

– Muscle spasms.

Most prevalent in lactating mares.

Sulphur (S)

Functions:

– Synthesis of amino acids.

– Hoof growth.

– Activates enzymes.

– A constituent of **insulin**.

Sources:

Most horse feed, including grass.

Deficiency signs:

– Poor hair.

– Poor skin and hoof condition.

ITQ 72

a. Which macro-minerals are important in the development of bone?

b. Which vitamin is also needed for bone growth?

c. Why is this?

ITQ 73 Why should bran not be fed to young horses?

ITQ 74

a. State three functions of sodium.

b. State three signs of sodium deficiency.

Trace Minerals

Iron (Fe)

Functions:

- Promotes the production of red blood cells and is essential to the formation of haemoglobin, which carries oxygen in the blood.
- Involved in functioning of the central nervous system.
- Activates enzymes.

Sources:

- Most natural feeds.
- Deep-rooted herbs, such as comfrey.
- Mineral blocks and supplements.

Deficiency signs:

- Anaemia, particularly if aggravated by heavy worm infestation.
- Fatigue.
- Reduced growth.

Iodine (I)

Functions:

- Essential in the formation of thyroxin, the hormone governing the body's metabolic rate.
- Promotes growth.
- Aids the reproductive processes.

Sources:

- Herbs.
- Seaweed.
- Grass.
- Mineral licks.
- Supplements.

Deficiency signs:

- Hypothyroidism (under-active thyroid gland).
- Swelling of the thyroid gland (goitre).
- Cell abnormalities.
- Infertility.
- Poor condition.
- Weakness in foals.

– Suppressed growth.
– Abnormal oestrus cycle.

Excessive levels of iodine may prove toxic.

Cobalt (Co)

Functions:
– A component of the B12 vitamin which helps to prevent anaemia.
– Promotes bacterial activity necessary for synthesis of B12.

Sources:
– Most feeds.
– Fresh herbage.
– Mineral blocks.

Deficiency signs:
– Impaired B12 production, which may lead to anaemia.
– Rough coat.
– Poor appetite.

Manganese (Mn)

Functions:
– Promote the healthy development of bone, hair, skin and hooves.
– Is specifically required for the formation of **chondroitin sulphate** in cartilage.

Sources:
– Fresh herbage.
– Good hay.
– Cereals.
– Mineral blocks.
– Supplements.

Deficiency signs:
Deficiencies are rare as normal feed rations provide adequate quantities. Where seen, they are as follows:
– Bone abnormalities.
– Problems with the reproductive system.
– Incoordination in youngsters.
– Implicated in **developmental orthopaedic disease (DOD)**.

Zinc (Zn)

– Essential for carbohydrate and lipid metabolism.
– Along with copper, zinc is an essential component of antioxidant enzymes **(superoxide dismutase)**.

Sources:
– Fresh herbage.

  – Good hay.
  – Cereals.
  – Mineral blocks.
  – Supplements.

Deficiency signs:
As with manganese, deficiencies are rare as normal feed rations provide adequate quantities. Where seen, they are as follows:
  – Suppressed appetite.
  – Reduced growth.
  – Skin problems.
  – Implicated in developmental orthopaedic disease (DOD).

Copper (Cu)
Functions:
  – Involved in bone, cartilage, elastin and hair formation.
  – Promotes utilization of iron.
  – Involved in synthesis of haemoglobin.
  – Involved in melanin synthesis (coat colour).

Sources:
  – High levels in seed products such as linseed.
  – Various feedstuffs grown in soil containing the correct levels of copper.

Deficiency signs:
Deficiencies are rare as normal feedstuffs provide adequate quantities, but would show as:
  – Reduced growth and in youngsters, developmental orthopaedic disorder (DOD).
  – De-pigmentation of the coat may occur.
  – Diarrhoea.
  – Poor performance.
Availability (uptake/utilization) is reduced by high levels of molybdenum and iron.

Molybdenum (Mo)
Function:
  – Enzyme reactor.

Sources:
  – Grass, hay.

Deficiency signs:
  – Not seen.

Selenium (Se)
Functions:
  – Acts as an antioxidant as a component of the enzyme **glutathione peroxidase**.

- When utilized in conjunction with vitamin E, considered to help prevent cell damage.
- Is sometimes given to horses suffering or known to suffer from exertional rhabdomyolysis (azoturia), as implicated in some cases, although its effect is not proven.

Sources:
- Fresh herbage.
- Linseed.
- supplements.

Deficiency signs:
- Weak foals.
- Anaemia.
- Joint abnormalities.
- In some cases, azoturia.

Note: vitamin E and selenium supplements are very useful for high-performance horses, but should be given with care. *Selenium is toxic in abnormal dosage.* Excessive hair loss and hoof deformities are signs that the horse has ingested toxic levels of selenium.

ITQ 75 Which minerals are concerned with the maintenance of tissue fluids and acid/base balance?

ITQ 76
a. Which mineral is essential in the formation of thyroxine?

b. State two sources of this mineral.

SUPPLEMENTS

To ensure a good balance of vitamins and minerals in the diet it may occasionally be necessary to use vitamin and mineral supplements. Some common-sense measures relating to supplementation are as follows.

1. Add 25–100 g (1–4 oz) of common salt (depending on work rate, temperature and humidity) to one feed per day, in addition to the basal levels of sodium and chlorine in the diet. The more a horse sweats, the greater his need for salt.

2. Provide a salt and mineral block in the stable. (This also serves to occupy the stabled horse.)

3. Grow a herb strip in the field. Herbs are very deep-rooting and will draw up essential minerals from the soil.

4. Have pasture tested to show up deficiencies of particular minerals related to soil content. The deficiencies can then be corrected by adding to the diet accordingly. In the longer term, correct any soil deficiencies in the macro-nutrients magnesium, potassium and phosphorus, as well as the soil pH, with the use of fertilizers and lime. This is a particularly important aspect of grassland management on a stud where growing youngstock graze.

5. Compound feeds such as cubes and coarse mixes are specially blended to maintain constant and correct nutrient levels appropriate to need, being fortified with the necessary minerals, vitamins and trace elements. No additional supplements should be necessary when these are fed at or near to a manufacturer's recommended level.

When supplements have to be purchased, it is important to choose what is suitable for your horse's particular needs from the wide range available on the market. Some products offer a balance of all the necessary vitamins and minerals (in which case, one should be mindful of point 5 above, to avoid unwittingly over-supplementing), whereas others specialize in the provision of micro-nutrients to correct or improve specific conditions. For example **electrolyte** supplements provide a balance of the minerals lost when a horse sweats. Given the increasing popularity of equestrian sports that require significant exertion on the horse's part, it is worth looking at electrolytes in a little more detail.

Normal metabolism and cellular functions can only continue in the presence of the correct balance of fluids and electrolytes. Electrolytes are substances which conduct electricity through their **ions**. Ions are atoms with either a positive electrical charge (a **cation**) or a negative electrical charge (an **anion**). There must be a balance between anions and cations to ensure electrical neutrality and therefore normal cell function.

The most important electrolytes in equine metabolism are sodium and chlorine (obtained from common salt), potassium, calcium, magnesium, phosphorus and the trace elements iron, copper, zinc, cobalt, selenium, sulphur and iodine. The three electrolytes that are lost to the greatest extent in sweat are sodium, potassium and chlorine. (Electrolyte replacement is dealt with in Chapter 7.)

Another condition that can be improved by appropriate supplements is poor hoof quality. In addition to a good quality protein source in the diet, supplementation of biotin, methionine and zinc may be indicated.

In various circumstances where it is considered that the effective metabolism of proteins needs to be supported, the amino acids lysine, trytophan and methionine, may be given in supplements.

Other supplements commonly given to aid digestion are yeast and various probiotics. Stress, arising from factors such as travel and competition, or antibiotic therapy, can lead to changes in the balance of the bacteria, yeasts and fungi that colonize within the gut, and even to various levels of depletion. This can result in colic, loss of performance and condition, and digestive upsets such as diarrhoea.

Yeast, supplemented in the form of a highly concentrated yeast culture, enhances the gut's own yeast levels and produces metabolites which promote the growth of other beneficial microflora. Yeast can improve the digestibility of dry matter and fibre, which increases nutrient availability to the horse.

Probiotics are produced from naturally occurring micro-organisms They are designed to enhance the microbial population within the gut and therefore improve digestion and prevent digestive upset. Since the different strains of bacteria within the gut perform different functions, a multi-strain probiotic will be of greater benefit than a single-strain one.

Over-supplementation

Although considered, appropriate use of supplements can be very benefi- cial, any type of supplement should be given only after investigation has established a need for it. Correct management and good feeding, especially if using compound feeds, will minimize the need for supplements. As a result of overdosing, performance can be impaired, toxic levels may be reached and the horse will become ill. As mentioned earlier, many minerals interact with each other and each one can affect the action of another. This makes the need for the right balance in the diet very important.

ITQ 77

a. What are probiotics?

b. Give two examples of occasions when a horse might benefit from them.

CHAPTER SUMMARY

A balanced diet specific to individual requirements is essential if the horse is to stay healthy and perform at his best. In this chapter we have examined the nutrients needed by the horse, and the functions and sources of those nutrients.

Next, we will look at the digestive system and the way in which the nutrients are utilized by the horse to produce energy.

CHAPTER 4

EQUINE DIGESTION

The aims and objectives of this chapter are to explain:

- The anatomy of the digestive tract.
- The process of digestion.

A detailed description of the digestive tract can be found in Book 1 of this series; *Anatomy and Physiology*. Here, we will look at the digestive tract and its function in outline.

THE DIGESTIVE TRACT

The function of the digestive tract to process all feedstuffs and assimilate as many nutrients from them as is possible. Having done this, all waste matter is excreted or defecated from the body.

As mentioned earlier, the horse's digestive tract has evolved to cope with large quantities of fibre, mainly cellulose found in grass and grass products such as hay and haylage. Based on the anatomy of his digestive tract, the horse is classified as a **non-ruminant herbivore**. Whereas the gut of a carnivore is relatively short, the gut of a herbivore is long because it deals with cellulose, which is relatively difficult to digest and therefore needs to be held in the digestive tract for longer.

The equine digestive system consists of the **foregut** – mouth, pharynx, oesophagus, stomach and small intestines, and the **hind gut** – caecum, large colon, small colon, rectum and anus. The **pancreas** lies in close proximity to, and interacts with, the small intestine.

THE FOREGUT
The Mouth
Lips. The upper lip is very strong and mobile and is used to sort and grasp the food.

Incisors. These are cutting teeth used to bite the food.

Molars. These grinding teeth at the back of the jaw are used to chew the food.

Mandibular, parotid and sublingual glands. These are arranged in pairs and produce **saliva**, which warms, wets and lubricates the food to aid its movement down the digestive tract. As it contains bicarbonate, saliva is slightly alkaline. This is important because saliva helps to buffer the acids produced in the stomach as a natural consequence of digestion. Approximately 10–12 litres (about 2½ gallons) of saliva is produced daily. Saliva is produced in response to the chewing action – the amount produced is directly proportional to the number of chews. Equine saliva does not have any significant activity of the enzyme **salivary amylase** and recent work suggests that any **low activity** present is likely to be bacterial in origin.

Tongue. Forms the food into a **bolus** and passes the bolus to the back of the mouth (the **oropharynx**).

The Pharynx (Throat)

The pharynx is the cavity behind the mouth through which food passes on its way to the oesophagus. The food passes over the tracheal opening, which is protected by the epiglottis.

The **epiglottis** is a small cartilage at the root of the tongue, which covers the opening of the windpipe (trachea). The epiglottis is depressed during swallowing to prevent food or water entering the trachea.

The Oesophagus

The oesophagus is a tube approximately 1.2–1.5 m (4–5 ft) long (depending on the size of the horse or pony) which passes down the back of the trachea along the left-hand side of the neck. It passes down through the chest between the lungs, through the **diaphragm** (a muscle which separates the chest from the abdomen), into the abdominal cavity and to the stomach. No digestion occurs within the oesophagus.

The Stomach

When empty the stomach is relatively small, approximately the size of a rugby ball, but it can expand to contain 9–18 litres (2–4 gallons). Food is allowed into the stomach by a small ring muscle called the **cardiac sphincter**. This valve prevents food from passing backwards out of the stomach and can withstand great pressure. As a result it is very rare for horses to regurgitate food and they cannot physically be sick or belch.

The stomach is divided into four regions:

1. **The oesophageal region**. This acts as a holding area – there are no glands here and the food matter is pH neutral.

2. **The cardiac region**. Glands in this region produce mucus to protect the stomach lining from the effects of hydrochloric acid.

3. **The fundic region**. This is the main body of the stomach, containing three types of cells:
   Parietal or border cells – secrete hydrochloric acid.
   Neck chief cells – secretes mucus.

Body chief cells – secretes enzymes.

The food is highly acidic in the fundic region of the stomach.

4. **The pyloric region**. Pyloric glands secrete mucus and a small amount of protein- digesting enzymes. The food matter is very acidic in this area.

As food arrives in the stomach it stimulates the release of gastric juices and hydrochloric acid; 10–30 litres ($2^1/_4$–$6^3/_4$ gallons) of gastric juices are produced daily. Key constituents of the gastric juices are:

- **Pepsin.** This enzyme is secreted as **pepsinogen** in the gastric juices and is converted to pepsin by the hydrochloric acid present. Pepsin breaks down proteins into **peptones** and **protoeses**.

- **Hydrochloric acid.** Acidifies the food, has an anti-bacterial action and converts pepsinogen to pepsin.

- In foals, **rennin** coagulates milk.

Once the food is sufficiently acidic it leaves the stomach, regulated by another ring muscle, the **pyloric sphincter**, to enter the first section of the small intestine. At this stage it is known as **chyme**.

The horse's stomach is designed to remain partially full at all times; most food passes out of the stomach within forty-five minutes, whilst some remains for approximately two hours.

Note: As the horse's stomach is so small in relation to his overall size, it is tempting to feed too much at a time. It is better to feed to slightly below appetite, taking into account the volume capacity of the stomach. Divide his daily ration into as many small feeds as is practical.

The Small Intestine

This is the major site for the breakdown of concentrated food such as starch, lipids and protein, and for the absorption of nutrients.

The small intestine lies in coils close to the small colon and moves quite freely in the abdomen, except for its attachment at the stomach and caecum. The lining of the intestine is covered with small hair-like **villi,** which give a huge surface area to aid absorption. Between the villi are three types of gland:

1. **Intestinal glands (Crypts of Lieberkuhn)** – specialized glands found throughout the small intestine. They secrete large numbers of enzymes including:

   Aminopeptidases, which convert peptides into amino acids.

   Sucrase, which converts sucrose into glucose and fructose.

Lactase, which converts lactose to glucose and galactose.

Maltase, which breaks maltose down into glucose.

Intestinal lipase, which converts fats to fatty acids and glycerol.

2. **Duodenal glands (Bruner's glands)** – found in the duodenum. These secrete an alkaline solution.

3. **Peyer's patches** – found throughout the small intestine, these are accumulations of lymphoid tissue, the function of which is to produce antibodies and control bacterial populations.

Food is passed through the intestines by involuntary muscular contractions called **peristalsis**. The gut wall consists of a layer of longitudinal muscle and a layer of circular muscle. These layers work antagonistically to push the food in one direction.

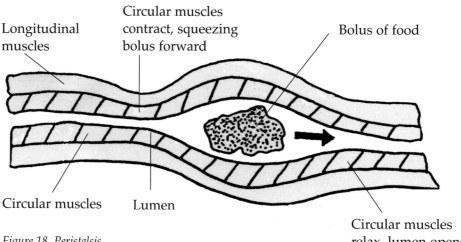

Figure 18 Peristalsis

The small intestine consists of three parts, the **duodenum**, the **jejunum** and the **ileum**.

The duodenum is approximately 1 m (3 ft 3 in) long and forms an 'S' shaped bend. Into it flows **bile**, secreted by the liver, and **pancreatic juices**, secreted by the pancreas.

The jejunum, the second part of the small intestine, is approximately 20 m (66 ft) long. Here, amino acids, vitamins, minerals and glucose are absorbed into the bloodstream. Lipids are digested and then re-assimilated within the epithelial cells of the gut into triglycerides. These triglycerides are then packaged up, together with protein and cholesterol, before they enter the circulation to be distributed around the body.

The ileum, the final part of the small intestine, is approximately 2 m (6 ft 6 in) long.

Mesentery tissue loosely supports the intestines and supplies them with blood vessels, lymphatics and nerves. The duodenum, jejunum and ileum have a volume capacity of approximately 50 litres (11 gallons).

ITQ 78 On average, how long does it take for food to pass through the horse's stomach?

ITQ 79 Name two substances secreted into the stomach in the presence of food and state the function of each.

ITQ 80 What is peristalsis?

THE PANCREAS

The pancreas is a lobulated gland, which lies behind the stomach, alongside the duodenum. It has two main functions:

1. To produce the hormones **insulin** and **glucagon**, which are concerned with the maintenance of the blood-glucose level. These hormones are produced by small masses of special cells interspersed throughout the pancreas called **'islets of Langerhans'**.

2. To produce **pancreatic juice**. This is secreted continually, but increases when food is present. Pancreatic juice contains sodium bicarbonate so it is alkaline, which reduces the acidity of the food. It also contains the enzymes **trypsinogen** and **chymotrypsinogen**. These are inactive until **enterokinase**, secreted by the duodenum, converts them to **trypsin** and **chymotrypsin**, which break proteins down into smaller fragments. Other enzymes in the pancreatic juice, **carboxypeptidase** and **aminopeptidase** then concert these fragments into amino acids. The pancreatic juice also contains the enzyme **amylase**, which breaks down starch into maltose.

The following Table 6 summarizes the different enzymes, their origins, the substances that they act upon (their substrates) and the end products.

ORIGIN	ENZYME	SUBSTRATE	END PRODUCT
Mouth	Salivary amylase	Starch	Maltose
Stomach	Pepsin	Proteins	Peptones and protoeses
Small intestine	Aminopeptidases	Peptides	Amino acids
Small intestine	Sucrase	Sucrose	Glucose and fructose
Small intestine	Lactase	Lactose	Glucose and galactose
Small intestine	Maltase	Maltose	Glucose
Small intestine	Intestinal lipase	Fats	Fatty acids and glycerol

Table 6 Digestive enzymes

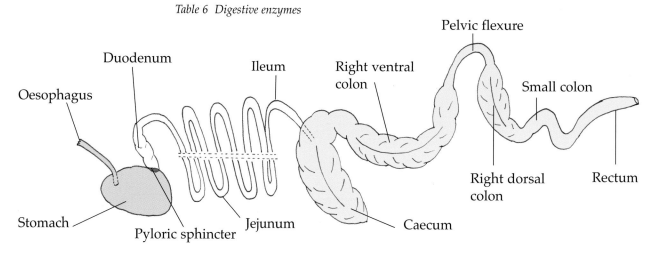

Figure 19 The digestive tract (a)

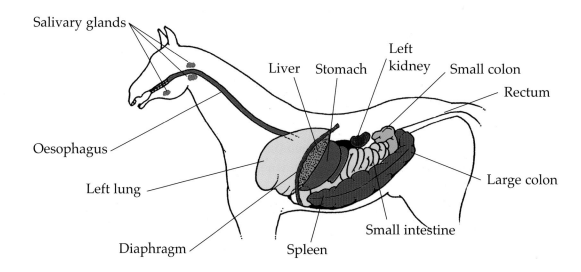

Figure 20 The digestive tract (b)

THE HIND GUT

The hind gut consists in the main of the large intestine, the major constituent parts of which are the caecum, the large and small colon and the rectum. The large intestine is the major site for the fermentation of fibre. Its main functions are:

- To provide the optimum environment for the micro-organisms that ferment the fibre.
- To digest any remaining soluble carbohydrates or starch.
- To absorb water and vitamins.

It is held in place only by its bulk and, because of flexures where the gut narrows and changes direction, it is prone to blockages.

The Caecum

Adjoining the final part of the small intestine, the ileum, is the first part of the large intestine, the caecum. Food reaches the caecum approximately three hours after a meal and remains in the large intestine for 36–48 hours. The caecum is capable of holding 36 litres (8 gallons). The **ileo-caecal valve** controls food coming into the caecum, where it is held before being passed on to the large colon on a 'top-up' basis.

The digestion of fibre begins in the caecum through the process of **fermentation.** This process is activated by a population of bacteria, yeasts, fungi and protozoa, specific to each particular type of feedstuff. The microbial population is continually changing depending on the diet (i.e. substrate available), and changes can take place within a time period of 24 hours.

Cellulose, hemicellulose and pectin, all components of fibre, are broken down to release **volatile fatty acids (propionic, butyric and acetic acids)**. These are used as an energy source by tissues.

The micro-organisms also synthesize essential vitamins.

A horse on a high roughage diet, such as one kept at grass, will have a large belly because of the bulk within the caecum.

The Large Colon

The first part of the large colon is known as the **right ventral colon**. This runs forward to the **sternal flexure**, where the diameter of the colon narrows and it turns back on itself. It continues backward to the **left ventral colon**, running along the left side of the horse to the pelvic region.

Here, the colon turns into the **pelvic flexure**, where the diameter reduces to approximately 9 cm (3.5 in) before it expands again towards the diaphragm as the **left dorsal colon**. It makes its final turn at the **diaphragmatic flexure**, forming the **right dorsal colon**, narrows and becomes the small colon.

The large colon is 3–4 m (9 ft 9 in–13 ft) long and holds approximately 82 litres (18 gallons) by volume. There are bacteria in the large colon, which continue the fermentation of cellulose.

The Small Colon

The third and final part of the large intestine has a much reduced diameter and, although about 3–4 m (9 ft 9 in–13 ft) long – a similar length to the large colon –it is capable of holding only about 14 litres (3 gallons). It lies intermingled with the jejunum and can move quite freely, making it susceptible to twisting. Water and nutrients are extracted through the walls of the small colon.

Further water is then extracted in the rectum, where the waste materials are formed into faeces to be expelled through the anus.

Note: The horse's digestive tract has a great capacity to ferment fibre; the hind gut can deal with large quantities of fibre-containing roughage. However, while the foregut can deal with small quantities of concentrated feed, the overall design of the digestive tract renders the horse susceptible to problems if too much concentrated feed is given, because of the possibility of blockages caused by partially digested food and consequential twisting.

> ITQ 81 Name three sets of glands found throughout the small intestine and state the functions of each.

> ITQ 82 Which digestive enzymes are present in pancreatic juice?

> ITQ 83
> a. On average, for how long does food remain in the caecum?
>
> b. How is fibre digested?

CHAPTER SUMMARY

The horse evolved as a browsing herbivore, wandering and grazing, spending short periods feeding throughout most of the day and some of the night. The horse's digestive tract adapted to cope with succulent forages containing large amounts of water, fibre, soluble sugars and protein.

Domestication has brought with it a different style of feeding – feed times are restricted and concentrated and processed materials, such as starchy cereals and dried forages, are fed. While it is not always possible to mimic the feeding habits of the feral horse completely, keeping as close as practical to the way 'nature intended' will reduce the risk of dietary and psychological imbalance.

This approach, combined with an understanding of the anatomy and physiology of the horse's digestive tract, will allow you to feed horses appropriately and sympathetically, thereby minimizing the likelihood of digestive problems arising.

CHAPTER 5

FEEDSTUFFS

The aims and objectives of this chapter are to explain:

- The different categories of feedstuffs.
- How feedstuffs are cooked and prepared.
- The advantages and disadvantages of feeding 'straights' and compound feeds.
- The different types of forage available for horses.
- The nutritive values of various feedstuffs.
- The main rules of feeding and the reasons behind them.

THE VARIOUS TYPES OF FEED

First, we will examine the variety of feedstuffs available for horses. Information is given regarding the nutritional value of each type of feedstuff (and summarized in Table 7) but it should be remembered that feedstuffs are affected by the way in which they have been harvested, processed and stored. Adverse conditions, in particular damp and ageing, will reduce the quality and nutritional value of the feed. It must also be considered that all heat treatments and processing of grains affects the vitamin content. Vitamins C, K, B12, B6 and A are all completely lost.

Feedstuffs may be divided into the following categories.

Cereals. These are quite often the basis of the concentrate ration and include energy-giving foods such as oats, maize and barley. Cereals must be prepared in such a way as to improve digestibility. The methods of doing this include boiling, rolling, bruising, crimping or heat treatments such as micronizing or extrusion. These treatments make the starch more digestible to the enzymes in the small intestine. This has the beneficial effect of reducing the amount of starch reaching the large intestine; excessive starch in the large intestine can predispose to colic, laminitis and other digestive upsets.

Micronizing involves subjecting the grain to infra-red heat, which turns the moisture in the grain to steam, thus cooking the grain internally. The starch chains become unravelled, a process known as gelatinization, which makes the glucose to glucose bonds more accessible to the horse's digestive enzymes.

Food can also be gelatinized by the **'dry extrusion method'** – this involves subjecting the food to intense pressure and heat treatment, again gelatinizing the starch and making it much easier to digest.

Fed individually, cereals are classified as 'straights', as opposed to compound feeds, which are discussed later.

Protein feeds. These can be of plant origin, such as soya, beans, peas and linseed. Sometimes, in certain circumstances, it may be necessary or expedient to feed proteins of animal origin, such as dried milk. Generally speaking however, the feeding of animal-derived proteins should be avoided, as it is not compatible with the evolved physiology of the horse.

Bulk feeds. These include bran, sugar beer pulp, grass meal and chaff – although these are often also referred to as 'straight feeding stuffs' since the term 'bulk feeding stuff' may be perceived as detracting from their nutritional value within a ration.

Compound feeds. These include the range of cubes and coarse feeds which are mixtures of the constituents mentioned above.

Forages. Grass, hay, haylage and silage.

We will now examine these categories in more detail.

CEREALS
Oats

Oats have a relatively high starch content which is digested well in the small intestine. Oats are therefore digested relatively quickly, yielding glucose which is then available for energy production using the faster energy-generating biochemical pathways. Oats have an anecdotal reputation for having a 'heating' effect in some horses, although the exact mechanism for this remains unknown. Good quality oats are plump, shiny, free of dust, pale yellow in colour and smell sweet. Oats are generally 'bruised' to break the husk and improve digestibility. Once bruised, their feed value gradually decreases. Oats are at their most nutritious within three weeks of bruising.

Naked oats are a modern development of this traditional feed. As a result of modified plant breeding, the husk separates from the kernel during harvesting, leaving the grain clean. A kilogram of naked oats will therefore have higher energy and protein levels than a kilogram of conventional oats, of which some weight is made up of the husks. Therefore, a lesser weight of naked oats need to be fed to supply the same levels of energy in the diet and there is no need to crimp or roll naked oats.

Naked oats are intended as a feed for performance horses. They have a much higher oil content and can contain up to 27 per cent more energy than conventional oats, so great care must be taken when feeding them – they must be fed in smaller quantities. Also, as they have no husk the fibre content is reduced and therefore the forage level of the overall diet must be increased.

Good quality oats can comprise up to 90 per cent of the concentrate ration.

Barley

For some horses, barley has less of a 'heating' effect than oats. This may be related to the fact that uncooked barley is less digestible in the small intestine. Barley is traditionally used as a conditioning feed because of its high energy content. Barley can make up 50 per cent of the concentrate ration, but no more owing to its relatively low fibre content.

Barley grains are rounder and plumper than oats, with a clean and shiny appearance. Barley can be fed cooked and flaked or heat-treated (micronized). Whole barley can be soaked and boiled to provide a nutritious, conditioning feed.

Maize

Maize is a high-energy feed containing little fibre. It is normally fed cooked and 'flaked' and should be a bright golden colour, crisp and clean. Normally maize does not make up more than 25 per cent of the ration. Maize should never be fed uncooked as the starch will not be digested in the small intestine, with large quantities thus reaching the hind gut.

Note: Oats, maize and barley have poor calcium to phosphorous ratios and all are low in the essential amino acids lysine and methionine. These deficiencies can be rectified by feeding a supplement and/or balancer, as discussed later in this chapter

PROTEIN FEEDS
Linseed

Linseed is the seed of the flax plant. The linseeds are small, flat, dark brown and shiny. Linseed is high in protein but has a relatively low lysine content and thus, despite its actual protein levels, it is not considered to be a good quality protein source. However, linseed is high in oil, and therefore has a high energy value.

In its raw state, linseed contains prussic acid, which in large quantities is toxic to the horse. Therefore, by way of preparation, the seeds should always be soaked overnight. Then, change the water, bring to the boil and simmer for approximately one hour. The resulting jelly and liquid can be separated if desired to make nourishing mashes. Linseed can also be micronized, a process which destroys the anti-nutritive factors, and fed as a meal without the need to soak.

Linseed is also processed to produce a hard cake and small particles are often included in coarse mixes.

Beans and Peas

Beans and peas have high protein and energy content. They may be fed crushed, split or micronized. **Soya bean meal** provides a rich source of high quality protein as it has a high lysine and threonine content.

ITQ 84

a. List two food treatment methods designed to improve the digestibility of starches.

b. What is the main nutritional disadvantage of these treatments?

ITQ 85 What do you think is the main nutritional disadvantage of feeding straights?

BULK (INTERMEDIATE) FEEDS
Bran

Bran is the offal from wheat and should appear as broad flakes, pink and sweet smelling. It has a low energy value and used to be considered useful for horses in rest. It may have a laxative effect when used as a mash. Generally speaking, bran is not much fed to horses in Great Britain nowadays as there are many nutritionally superior low-energy, non-heating feedstuffs available.

The crude protein level of bran appears to be high but is not of a high quality or easily digested. The calcium to phosphorus ratio is poor so a calcium supplement such as limestone flour or alfalfa (also known as lucerne) must be given to horses fed bran. Because of the poor calcium:phosphorus ratio, bran is particularly unsuitable for young horses.

Sugar Beet

Sugar beet is a useful non-heating and highly digestible source of energy and fibre. Sugar beet is a bi-product of the sugar extraction industry and when not supplemented with molasses has a low sugar content. Molassed sugar beet, by comparison, has a relatively high sugar content. The fibre content of sugar beet is highly digestible, being fermented in the large intestine. Sugar beet is often referred to as a **superfibre**.

Sugar beet is usually fed well soaked and large quantities of dry beet must never be fed as it will absorb water from the intestines, swell and cause colic. It is, however, common for compound feeds to contain small quantities of unsoaked sugar beet. Shredded sugar beet must be soaked in twice its weight of water for 12 hours; cubes for 24 hours in three times their weight of water. Sugar beet pellets are now also micronized to produce a product which requires only 10 minutes soaking.

Sugar beet pulp helps to correct an imbalance in the calcium to phosphorus level caused by the feeding of cereals, as it has a very good calcium to phosphorus ratio itself, providing a readily available source of calcium.

Chaff

Chaff consists of chopped hay, straw or alfalfa. This is often mixed with molasses to improve palatability, although this addition should not be used to disguise poor quality basic materials. Other additives may include limestone flour, garlic and herbs. Chaff aids digestion and encourages the horse to chew his food more thoroughly and, nutritionally, it is a better 'mixer' than bran. However, since chaff sometimes contains a high proportion of oat straw, its actual feed value can vary.

Alfalfa has a much higher nutritional value than simple hay- or straw-based chaffs and is often used as a feed in itself simply with a vitamin and mineral supplement.

COMPOUND FEEDS

Concentrate cubes and coarse mixes come under the heading of compound feeds that is, feeds blended from various ingredients to fulfil specific nutritional needs.

Cubes

Concentrate cubes are formulated to constitute the normal short feed rations, maintaining a constant and correct nutrient level appropriate to the requirements of the horse. Cubes are thus specially blended and fortified with vitamins and minerals to suit the specific and differing needs of the various types of horse. They are available in a number of forms:

Complete cubes (Hi-fibre) also contain the forage and concentrate rations, so are very high in fibre. They are useful for a horse who is unable to eat hay, possibly because of old age or a respiratory allergy. (For old horse with poor teeth, soaked complete cubes require less chewing than other feedstuffs.) However, despite their feed value, they can tend to provide a boring diet and succulents should be fed in addition.

Horse and pony cubes are non-heating, palatable concentrates for animals in ordinary work.

Stud cubes are variously designed to meet the needs of broodmares, their foals, stallions and youngstock. They maintain condition and fertility in mature stock through the inclusion of essential vitamins, minerals and trace elements. Those designed for youngstock place particular emphasis is placed on adequate levels of calcium to optimize growth and bone development. They can also be useful for building up a horse in poor condition.

Yearling cubes are specially formulated to follow on from creep feeds, providing the nutrient density that is ideal for bone and muscle development and sound healthy growth. They contain calcium, phosphorus and lysine.

Racehorse and **competition cubes** are designed to meet the needs of the high performance horse. They contain high levels of cereals and provide good quality proteins, rich in the amino acids lysine and methionine. Both racehorse and competition cubes must be guaranteed to be suitable for horses competing under FEI, BSJA and Jockey Club rules in respect of being free of 'non-normal nutrients'.

Protein concentrates are high protein pellets used in conjunction with other cereals and roughage.

Coarse Mixes

Coarse mixes are designed to make up the whole concentrate ration to be fed with the normal forage. You can mix a coarse mix with sugar beet pulp and chaff to wet the feed and bulk out the ration to satisfy the appetite.

Mixes contain a highly palatable mixture of cereals and other straight feeding stuffs or bulk feeds, with balanced levels of protein, minerals and trace elements.

Mixes vary in their nutrient content according to their specification and intended use. Horse and pony mixtures contain ingredients such as non-heating pellets, barley, maize, grass meal, molasses, alfalfa, linseed cake and bran. These non-heating mixes are usually marketed as 'Cool', 'Pasture' or 'Pony' mixes. Higher protein mixes also contain protein pellets, peas and beans and are usually called 'High Performance', 'Competition', 'High Profile' mixes, or similar, dependent upon the manufacturer. It is also possible to buy mixes specially designed for older horses – 'Veteran Mixes'.

Balancers

These are a cross between a feed and a vitamin and mineral supplement. As they are designed to be fed in relatively small amounts they are very nutrient-dense. In other words they usually have a higher energy and protein content per kilogram in relation to conventional mixes and cubes, as well as a higher concentration of vitamins and minerals. They are ideal to feed to horses who have access to plenty of grazing and forage and only require a small quantity of feed to maintain condition. Balancers can be tailored to accompany a high-forage diet, to complement cereals or alfalfa.

Advantages and Disadvantages of Compound Feeds

There are both advantages and disadvantages to using compound feeds.

Advantages:

- They are highly palatable and enjoyed by most horses – particularly the coarse mixes.

- Provided they are stored correctly and are used within their expiry date, the quality of the ingredients is normally guaranteed to be high. You would, however, need to check that the feed company does guarantee a constant nutritional value.

- The balance of nutrients is specific to the type of work each cube or mix is designed for. This makes it more difficult to over- or under-feed a particular nutrient.

- Owing to the inclusion of vitamins and minerals, extra supplements will not be necessary if the compound feeds are fed at the level recommended.

- Cubes have a long storage life, being more resistant to damp than cereals.

- They make it easier to measure out feed rations and save labour because no mixing is needed.

Disadvantages:
- Compound feeds need to be fed at the level recommended by the manufacturer concerned in order for the horse or pony to receive the requisite level of vitamins and minerals. In reality, many owners find that they feed significantly less, either because of the availability of grass or the metabolism of an individual. Under these circumstances, additional vitamin and mineral supplementation is often required.

- Some horses find cubes boring and go off their feed.

- A sick horse may find cubes unpalatable and will probably not be tempted to try them.

- It is not convenient to mix wormers or medicines in with cubes.

- Some non-heating coarse mixes may contain barley or similar cereals, which can prove unsuitable for certain types of pony.

- Cost has to be considered – compound feeds often work out expensive for large commercial yards.

ITQ 86 What is the main nutritional advantage of compound feeds?

ITQ 87 What external factors affect the nutritional value of feedstuffs?

FORAGE

The horse in his natural state obtains virtually all his nutritional requirements from grasses. In order for the horse to perform and expend high levels of energy it is necessary to feed concentrates. It is important, however, to appreciate that the competition diet is an artificial one and thus great care must be taken when feeding. Wherever possible, the horse's natural eating habits (grazing more or less continually) should be encouraged. The horse must receive at least one per cent of his bodyweight per day as forage. When not being grazed by the horse from the meadow or paddock, grass may be conserved in the form of hay, haylage and silage – although there will be some loss of nutrients during the process of conservation.

Hay

Good quality hay will provide an energy source on a slow release basis – the fibre is fermented for long periods (12–24 hours), resulting in a regular, even release of nutrients. This is what nature intended – as we have seen, the horse's gut is designed to ferment and digest large quantities of roughage.

Meadow hay is soft hay made from permanent pasture and containing a mixture of grasses, normally low in protein.

Seed hay is harder, coarser hay made from rye grass leys with higher protein levels. It is coarser than meadow hay because it is cut later, so greater lignification has occurred. This reduces its digestibility.

All hay should be cut when the grasses are flowering. If it is left too late the seed heads ripen and are lost. Since 80 per cent of nutrients are in the leaf, stemmy hay is of lower feed value as well as being more fibrous and difficult to digest. Hay must be sweet-smelling, mould-free and greenish in colour.

Minimizing Dust in Hay

All hay contains a certain amount of dust. Contaminants include fungal spores, bacteria, pollens, dust mites and other dust fragments. Exposure to these harmful contaminants may cause recurrent airway disease, respiratory hypersensitivity and infection. Steps must therefore be taken to minimize the horse's intake of dust to ensure good health and maximum performance. These steps include:

Soaking the hay to remove dust particles. Fungal spores will, however, survive the soaking so will still be ingested. Any dust particles not washed through will stick to the hay, which at least means they cannot escape into the air. The ingestion of dust and fungal spores would appear to be far less harmful than inhalation. *Excessive soaking* causes a loss of nutrient value, therefore hay should be soaked for approximately 10 minutes.

Steaming is more time-consuming and is often difficult when large quantities of hay are used. A large plastic dustbin may be used for steaming: pour boiling water onto the hay and replace the lid. Add boiling water periodically to keep the pressure of steam up for approximately 10 minutes. While steaming can help to reduce dust intake, it may reduce nutritional values to some extent.

Vacuuming the hay through a dust extractor machine is an effective way of removing contaminants. Having taken in the hay, it combs and vacuums it, delivering loose, clean material. The machine is fully portable but must be connected by a qualified electrician to a 20-amp single phase electricity supply.

The machine is relatively expensive but would be a valuable item of equipment in a large yard; in fact all horses and ponies would benefit greatly from the advantages of having 97 per cent of dust removed from their hay and straw. It should take about $2^{1}/_{2}$ minutes to process a bale but, in practice, the machine can prove rather more time-consuming.

Shaking up hay thoroughly, using a long-handled fork out of doors, allows dust fragments to be blown away. However, it is dangerous for handlers to breathe in large quantities of dust, as this can cause problems such as farmer's lung (hypersensitive pneumonitis). Therefore, a protective mask should be worn. Also, steps should be taken to ensure that the dust does not blow towards other personnel, or towards horses.

Haylage

Haylage is a compromise between hay and silage: grass is cut between heading and flowering, left to dry partially then baled and vacuum packed into tough plastic bags. When correctly processed, the anaerobic storage conditions encourage the production of lactic acid, which inhibits further fermentation as well as the activities of clostridia bacteria. The speed at which haylage is processed ensures minimal loss of nutrients and freedom from dust and fungal spores. So, although it is fairly expensive, it is an ideal forage for horses in hard, fast work or any horse with an allergic respiratory problem.

While haylage is very nutritious and highly palatable, it must always be used within three days of opening a bale. Once the tough outer bag has been torn the haylage starts to deteriorate.

Haylage should be fed to at least the same level (by weight) as hay and ideally in slightly larger amounts to compensate for its higher water content. The level of concentrates can then be reduced to compensate for the higher feed value of haylage. However, in reality, owners often reduce the quantity of haylage fed and maintain the level of concentrate feed. Therefore, because of the smaller quantities involved, boredom is often a problem in horses fed. This can be overcome by using a special haylage net, which has small openings, making it more difficult for the horse to pull the haylage out quickly.

Some manufacturers now produce a lower protein grade of haylage suitable for ponies, and 'high fibre' bagged forage made from grasses which have been allowed to mature for longer, resulting in more fibre and slightly less protein and energy.

ITQ 88 What is meant by a 'balancer' and in what circumstances are balancers used?

ITQ 89 Why is it essential to include as much fibre as possible in the horse's diet?

Hydroponic Grass

Hydroponic units allow grass, usually barley, to be grown in trays of water in specially heated and lit machines. This is a good way of providing fresh grass for horses, particularly in the winter. The grass is, however, very low in fibre so should not be used as the only forage feed.

Advantages of feeding hydroponic grass:
- It is useful if there is a shortage of land, e.g. no turnout during autumn and winter.
- It is a dust-free source of forage.
- It provides a good source of vitamin E and biotin.

Disadvantages of feeding hydroponic grass:
- Cost – the initial outlay for equipment and the running costs are high.
- Mould formation if the optimum growing conditions are not maintained.
- Increased labour.
- Reduced palatability – the grass tastes slightly bitter.

Dried Alfalfa (Lucerne)

Alfalfa is available in three forms; alfalfa pellets, chopped alfalfa (mixed with molasses) and alfalfa/straw blends.

High quality alfalfa crops are harvested as near as possible to the optimum nutritional stage, dried and specially cubed. Dried alfalfa provides energy and good quality protein.

Alfalfa also contains readily available minerals, particularly calcium. Dried alfalfa could, in theory, be fed as the sole forage source in terms of providing a dust-free ration, but in such quantities this would grossly oversupply both protein and calcium and be deficient in phosphorus. Alfalfa has a naturally high calcium:phosphorus ratio (5:1). Excessive protein and calcium intake may put greater stress on the horse's kidneys in removing the re-processed protein and excessive calcium from the body. In Britain, alfalfa is fed at levels up to 2–3 kg ($4^1/_2$ – $6^1/_2$ lb) per day as part of the bucket feed and in this form it adds to the nutritional value of the overall ration.

Silage

Silage is essentially grass that has been 'cut green' (just after heading and earlier than for haylage) and then sealed in bags, often in 'big bales'. Well-made silage must reach a pH of 4.5 as quickly as possible and contain at least 25 per cent dry matter to prevent the growth of harmful bacteria. While it is commonly fed to cattle, if used for horses silage must be fed cautiously, introducing very small quantities at first. In fact it is safest to avoid the use of big bale silage until more is known about the problems that can be caused when it is eaten by horses.

Botulism had not been frequently reported in horses until big bale silage started to be used as fodder. This condition is caused by the toxins of the bacteria *Clostridium botulinum,* which is present in the soil and is a fairly common contaminant of animal feedstuffs.

Once contaminated silage has been ingested, signs may show within three to seven days depending upon the quantities eaten. Signs include general weakness, difficulty in eating and progressive paralysis which results in the horse moving with a shuffling, stiff gait, dragging the toes along the ground. He may stand with his head and neck distended. Respiratory paralysis may occur, resulting in death.

Diagnosis is generally made upon examination of the feedstuffs. The vet may administer food, liquid paraffin and electrolytes via a stomach tube – this has proved helpful in the small percentage of cases that have survived.

Prevention of botulism involves never feeding contaminated/spoiled feedstuffs (of any sort) and only using big bale silage if the bag is intact, the pH level is 4.0–4.5 and there is a good aroma and no sign of moulds.

ITQ 90 What dietary imbalance may occur when feeding high levels of alfalfa?

ITQ 91 List the nutrients required by the horse and state which feedstuffs provide good levels of each nutrient.

	Crude Protein g/kg	Oil g/kg	Fibre g/kg	DE MJ/kg	Calcium g/kg	Phosphorus g/kg
Oats	96	45	100	11	0.7	3
Naked oats	112	87	25	15	0.6	3.5
Barley	95	18	50	12.8	0.06	3.3
Maize	86	38	25	14.2	0.02	3
Soya beans	440	10	62	13.3	2.4	6.5
Dried milk	340	0.6	0	15.1	10.5	9.8
Linseed	219	316	76	18.5	2.4	5.2
Bran	132	15	110	10.8	2.1	8.5
Sugar beet	90–120	1–6	130	7.5	6	0.7
Paddock coarse mix	85	3	150	9	1.2	0.5
Competition coarse mix	120	3.5	80	12.5	1.2	0.5
Stud coarse mix	140	37	62	12	13	7
Youngstock coarse mix	150	37	90	12.5	13	7
Veteran coarse mix	120	50	140	12.5	12	5
Horse & pony cubes	105	31	140	9	15	7
Racehorse cubes	140	58	60	13.0	6	5
Good hay	100	25	270	10.0	6.3	3.1
Average hay	75	25	300	8.0	5.0	2.5
Poor hay	45	25	360	7.0	2.0	1.2
Haylage	44	30	109	3.5	1.6	1.0
Silage	45	40	150	12.0	2.5	1.5
Chaff	40		260	8		
Dried alfalfa	150	17	230	9	18	2

Table 7 Nutritive values of various feedstuffs

FEEDING GUIDELINES

In the next chapter, we will discuss methods of rationing. Whatever methods are employed for calculating rations, whether scientific 'high-tech' or 'common sense low-tech', it is first essential to have knowledge of the underlying rules of feeding. These, and the key reasons behind them, are listed below.

1. **Feed plenty of roughage**

   a. There must never be less than 25 per cent roughage in the diet. The horse's intestine and caecum are specially designed to cope with a high-roughage diet – they contain many bacteria, yeasts and protozoa, which specialize in the fermentation of fibre including cellulose.

   b. Eating roughage alleviates boredom and helps maintain normal gut function.

2. **Feed little and often – try to mimic the eating habits of feral horses if possible**

   a. The horse's stomach is relatively small – approximately the size of a rugby ball. Divide feeds into several small feeds per day rather than one or two large feeds.

   b. The horse is naturally intended to be a 'trickle feeder'.

   c. Turn the horse out as much as possible – this enables him to graze and allows him to act as he would in feral conditions. This is one of the key points in avoiding behavioural problems with horses. Restricted eating habits lead to boredom and sometimes to the development of gastric (stomach) ulcers.

3. **Allow at least one and a half hours after feeding before working**

   a. A distended stomach will press on the diaphragm, preventing full inflation of the lungs.

   b. Digestion slows down during exercise because of the diversion of some of the blood supply from the gut to the muscles, resulting in a loss of nutrients and possibly colic.

4. **Feed all horses according to their individual needs, i.e. according to their breed, size, work, type, temperament, age, health and time of year**

   a. The bigger the horse, the more food is necessary for maintenance.

   b. A horse in hard work needs to be fed more to provide the necessary energy.

   c. Different temperaments affect the choice between 'heating' and 'non-heating' feedstuffs. A naturally 'fizzy' type will require a less heating diet than a more staid, cobby sort.

   d. Overfeeding often has worse consequences than underfeeding. Overfeeding can lead to laminitis, exertional rhabdomyolysis (azoturia), obesity and colic.

   e. Young growing horses require high protein levels.

f. If horses have access to grass, the quality and quantity of grass will vary with the seasons. During the winter, grass is of low feed value and horses use energy to keep warm, so feed levels should be increased. During spring, summer and early autumn, grass is often plentiful and high in nutrients. At this time feed levels can be reduced.

5. Keep feed levels ahead of workload

a. Cut down on energy-giving feeds the day before the rest day to prevent problems linked to an excess intake of carbohydrates, for example laminitis, exertional rhabdomyolysis and lymphangitis.

b. Try to lead out in hand or turn out on a rest day.

c. In the event of unplanned rest, such as through lameness or extreme bad weather, cut out all energy-giving feeds and replace with extra forage. Do not feed a lot of bran mashes because bran inhibits the horse's uptake of calcium. It is more sensible to feed a balanced ration of a non-heating compound feed such as horse and pony cubes.

d. If fed energy-giving food, horses at rest will probably become less manageable and generally 'full of themselves'.

6. Water must always be available

a. Fresh clean water must always be available except in some competition circumstances, such as immediately before the cross-country phase of a horse trial. However, it is important that the horse has not been allowed to get thirsty during the day, prior to his cross-country round.

b. Should a thirsty horse take a long drink immediately after eating, the water will pass over the contents of the stomach because of the 'J' shape of the stomach. (It used to be thought that food would be washed out of the stomach before the digestive juices secreted by the stomach lining were able to start the process of digestion but this is not so.) Many horses will take a few sips whilst eating; this is quite normal.

c. Water should be offered to horses at least every two hours on long journeys.

7. Introduce changes in the diet gradually

The bacteria in the gut are adept at fermenting and synthesizing nutrients from specific types of feedstuffs. Therefore, any sudden changes will result in impartial digestion because of a lack of a particular population of bacteria. This could result in a wastage of nutrients, diarrhoea and, possibly, colic.

8. Feed only good quality feedstuffs

a. Buy only good quality fodder and then ensure the best storage conditions. Store in dry, vermin-proof bins, always using up existing feedstuffs before adding newly opened feed.

b. Some feedstuffs such as bran are prone to absorbing moisture from the atmosphere. Purchase these in small quantities only.

c. Keep all buckets, mangers and scoops scrupulously clean.

d. Be aware that certain feedstuffs have a 'use-by' date – e.g. cereals and compound mixes.

9. Feed something succulent every day

a. This helps to keep the stabled horse interested in his food and provides variety.

b. It also provides a natural source of vitamins and minerals. Grass is an ideal green feed but if the horse is stabled, carrots or picked grass may be fed.

10. Keep to regular feed times

Horses enjoy a routine because they are creatures of habit. It can be stressful to the horse if an expected feed doesn't arrive.

ITQ 92 Which feeding guidelines help to prevent boredom?

ITQ 93 State two possible consequences of overfeeding.

ITQ 94 Why is it important to introduce changes to the diet gradually?

CHAPTER SUMMARY

In this chapter we've looked at the main range of feedstuffs available. You'll have seen the many advertisements of the different feed companies promoting the wide range of compound feeds that are available. It is important to appreciate that the nutritive values of feedstuffs vary according to the way in which they are harvested, processed and stored. This is particularly relevant to forage feeds such as hay.

This chapter concluded with a look at the feeding guidelines which should form the basis upon which every horse is fed. Having discussed feedstuffs, we'll now look at rationing.

CHAPTER 6

RATIONING

The aims and objectives of this chapter are to explain:

- How to calculate a daily feed ration.
- How to find out the information needed to calculate the ration.
- Factors to consider in terms of costs of feedstuffs.
- How to monitor the horse's condition.

CALCULATING A FEED RATION

When calculating how much to feed, it is necessary to take into account whether you are feeding for **maintenance** or **production.** Feeding for maintenance enables the horse's essential processes such as tissue repair, growth, digestion and respiration to occur without a loss of condition. Normally a horse can be maintained on a forage-only ration with the exception of additional micro-nutrients. Feeding for production may be split into the following categories:

- growth
- pregnancy
- lactation
- work
- repair
- conditioning.

In these cases, the horse requires energy-giving foods to provide an immediate source of energy as well as to replenish the body's energy stores such as muscle and liver glycogen and adipose fat stores. Where the diet is insufficient as a source of energy, the horse will draw on bodily reserves, ultimately losing condition.

The **digestible energy (DE)** content of feedstuffs is measured in **megajoules (MJ)** or, in the USA, as **megacalories (Mcal)**. To convert between these units, the following equations are used:

$$MJ = 4.183 \times Mcal$$
$$Mcal = MJ \div 4.183$$

It is necessary to know the nutritive values of different feedstuffs when calculating rations. Table 7 (see previous chapter) gives this information.

As with people, there is a great deal of variation in the daily energy requirement between individual horses, even when they are of a similar size and weight and undertaking a similar level of work. For this reason, when calculating rations, common sense plays a large part. Constant observation of the horse's condition will help you to decide whether the horse is in energy balance and thus receiving the right amount and type of feedstuffs. There are, however, several steps that can be taken to ensure that the horse is receiving a fully balanced diet.

In the first place, the nature of the horse's work will determine how much of the ration will be forage and how much will be concentrates (see Table 8).

Work Type	Intensity of exercise	Forage %	Concentrates %
Maintenance		80–100	20–0
Light Work/ Slow Hacking	Low	70	30
Schooling/ Light Jumping	Low	70	30
Medium Work	Low/High	50	50
Hard Work	Low/High	50	50
Very Fast Work	High	40	60

Table 8 Ratios of forage to concentrates

Calculating a ration involves finding out:
1. The horse's bodyweight.

2. The maximum amount of food a horse of this weight should be fed daily.

3. How much energy is needed daily for maintenance.

4. How much energy is needed daily for production

5. The correct level of protein needed in the diet.

These calculations can be made using information provided and equations formulated by nutritional analysts. The formulae may seem complicated at first but, if followed carefully and logically, it will become apparent how a balanced ration can be calculated.

ITQ 95 In terms of feeding for production, list the six categories.

ESTIMATION OF BODYWEIGHT

Bodyweight can be calculated or estimated in several ways:

Weighbridges provide an accurate way of finding out how much a horse weighs. Remember, if using a commercial weighbridge, that horses do not feel safe walking on sheet metal. To counteract this problem you could weigh the lorry or car and empty trailer first then put the horse in and weigh again. Alternatively, place a sheet of rubber matting on the bridge. Some veterinary practices have a specially designed equine weighbridge.

Weighing machines specially designed for horses are useful in large yards, particularly those associated with racing. Horses may be weighed before and after a race to assess the level of weight loss and dehydration.

Tables of weights. give approximate bodyweights of various types of horse and pony (see Table 9).

Type	Height (hh)	Approximate Weight	
		kg	lb
Pony	13.0	300	660
Large Pony	14.2	425	935
Small Hunter	15.2	500	1,100
Medium Hunter	16.0	575	1,265
Large Hunter	16.3	650	1,430
Draught/Shire	17.0	1,000	2,200

Table 9 Approximate bodyweights

Weightapes are used around the girth and give the approximate bodyweight. They can be purchased from equestrian suppliers.

Girth and body length measurements. can be used to make approximate calculations of weight. Measure around the heart girth (G) and from the point of shoulder to the point of buttock (L) and use the following equations:

$$\frac{G \text{ (cm)} \times G \text{ (cm)} \times L \text{ (cm)}}{11877} = \text{Bodyweight (kg)}$$

$$\frac{G \text{ (in)} \times G \text{ (in)} \times L \text{ (in)}}{330} = \text{Bodyweight (lb)}$$

DETERMINING MAXIMUM DAILY FEED

This is related to bodyweight – a horse can generally eat only up to 2.5 per cent of his bodyweight daily. He does not *have* to eat to this maximum however and many will only eat up to 2 per cent of bodyweight daily. Maximum daily feed can be calculated as follows:

(Bodyweight (kg) ÷ 100) x 2.5 = Maximum daily amount of food (dry matter kg)

Example: A 15.2 hh small hunter weighs approximately 500 kg as taken from the weight table. (500 ÷ 100) x 2.5 = 12.5 kg (28 lb)

This means that 12.5 kg (28 lb) in total of hay and concentrates is fed per day, the ratio of which is determined by the sort of work the horse is doing.

Note: Feedstuffs should be weighed dry to improve accuracy when calculating the provision of nutrients. All weights quoted throughout the text are **dry weights**.

IN-TEXT ACTIVITY

Using the formulae of girth and body length measurements, select two horses known to you and calculate their weights. Compare the calculated weights with the weights given in Table 9.

CALCULATING ENERGY NEEDED DAILY FOR MAINTENANCE

The recognized formula according to the National Research Council (1989) is:

For horses of 200–600 kg:
$$DE \ (Mcal[1]/day) = 1.4 + (0.03 \times bw[2] \text{ in kg})$$

For horses of more than 600 kg:
$$DE \ (Mcal/day) = 1.82 + (0.0383 \times bw \text{ in kg}) - (0.000015 \times bw \times bw)$$

Examples to find out Mcal needed per day for maintenance:
1. For 500 kg horse: 1.4 + (0.03 x 500) = 16.4 Mcal/day
   Remember – do the calculation within the brackets separately:
   0.03 x 500 = 15, so 1.4 + 15 = 16.4.

2. For 750 kg horse: 1.82 + (0.0383 x bw in kg) – (0.000015 x bw x bw) = 22.11, or: 1.82 + 28.72 = 30.54 – 8.43 = 22.11

---

[1] As explained on page 115, to convert Mcal/day to MJ/day multiply by 4.183

[2] bw – bodyweight

ITQ 96 Calculate the Mcal/day maintenance requirements of the following horses:

a. 400 kg horse   1.4 + (0.03 X 400) =   Mcal/day.

b. 625 kg horse   1.82 + (0.0383 x 625) – (0.000015 x 625 x 625)
                                        =   Mcal/day.

c. 800 kg horse...

d. 550 kg horse...

ITQ 97 Convert all the Mcal/day in ITQ 96 to MJ/day.

a. 400 kg horse.

b. 625 kg horse.

c. 800 kg horse.

d. 550 kg horse.

CALCULATING ENERGY NEEDED FOR DAILY PRODUCTION

This is based on the following requirements:

Working

Light work	1.25 x maintenance
Medium work	1.50 x maintenance
Hard work	2.00 x maintenance

Stallion

(in the breeding season)	1.25 x maintenance

Pregnant Mares

1–8 months	As for maintenance
9 months	1.11 x maintenance
10 months	1.13 x maintenance
11 months	1.20 x maintenance

Example: 15.2 hh small hunter in hard work, being ridden daily and hunting once a week:

Weight 500 kg, therefore DE requirements for maintenance are:

$(MJ/kg) = 4.183 \times (1.4 + (0.03 \times 500))$

$= 4.183 \times 16.4$

$= 68.6$

And so taking into consideration the work element:

$= 2 \times maintenance$

$= 2 \times 68.6$

$= 137 \, MJ/day$

ITQ 98 How is the digestible energy value of food measured?

ASCERTAINING THE CORRECT PROTEIN LEVEL

The crude protein level required by a horse varies according to the differing performance functions. The requirements are shown in Table 10 as percentages of the total food requirement.

	Protein in ration
Work:	
Light/medium work	7.5–8.5%
Hard/fast work	9.5–10%
Lactation and pregnancy:	
First three months lactation	14%
Next three months lactation	12%
Final third of pregnancy	11%
Growth:	
Suckling foal	17%
Weaned foal	15%
Yearling to eighteen months	13%
Eighteen months to two years	11%
Two to four years	10%

Table 10 Necessary crude protein levels

FORMULATING FEED RATIONS

So far, we have been concerned with the criteria for calculating how much to feed in order to provide the right level of nutrients. We have examined the different nutritional requirements of individual horses according to their size and workload and discussed the various types of feedstuffs and their nutritional value. We now move on to actually formulate the rations for each individual type of horse. Having put together a ration for any horse, it is essential that its effectiveness is constantly monitored and alterations made as necessary.

Note: The feedstuffs and quantities suggested in the following calculations are given by way of working examples. While they offer guidance to the process of calculating suitable rations, they are also designed to highlight the approximation and choices that are part and parcel of the process of arriving at a ration to suit the individual horse.

EXAMPLE OF A FEED RATION

By way of example, we'll now plan the feed ration of a 16.3 hh Irish Draught x Thoroughbred in hard work aiming for a three-day event. The horse has tendency to 'hot up', resulting in slight loss of condition during training.

We need to make the following calculations.

1. **Bodyweight.** Use table of weights = 650 kg.

2. **Maximum daily food intake.** (2.5 per cent of bodyweight)
   (650 kg ÷ 100) x 2.5 = 16.25 kg dry matter.

3. **Energy required for maintenance:** 4.183 x (1.4 + (0.03 x 650)) MJDE daily
   = 87.4 MJ/day.

4. **Energy for production:** three-day eventing = 2 x maintenance requirement
   Therefore total energy requirement = 2 x 87.4 = 175 MJ/day.

5. **Protein requirement:** between 9 and 10 per cent is necessary for hard, fast work. If we assume that this horse will eat to an appetite of 2.5% bodyweight, his dry matter intake will be 16.25 kg per day.

   Using Table 8 (earlier this chapter), a horse in hard work should receive at least 50 per cent of his total dry matter in the form of hay, and therefore the remaining 50 per cent from concentrates:

Kg/day from hay	16.25 x 0.5 =	8 kg
Kg/day from concentrates	16.25 x 0.5 =	8 kg
		16 kg.

Using the tabular extract below, we see that average hay contains 8 MJDE/kg. Therefore, 8 kg hay per day will give (8 x 8) 64 MJ per day.

Subtracting this from the total energy requirement of 175 MJ/day leaves an energy deficit of 111 MJ to be fulfilled by a suitable concentrate feed. Referring to Table 7 again, naked oats, for example, contain 15 MJDE/kg. Therefore, 111 MJDE will be obtained from (111÷15) 7.4 kg of naked oats per day:

Thus the horse would need to be fed 8 kg of average hay and 7.4 kg of naked oats per day to satisfy his energy requirements and this total quantity (15.4 kg) lies close to but within his expected daily appetite of 16.25 kg.

In practice the quantity of naked oats could be reduced slightly (and the energy requirements supplemented) by the addition of either alfalfa chaff or sugar beet to add variety.

If the hay were of the best quality one would also be able to make downward adjustments to the amount of concentrates being fed.

	Weight fed per day kg	Crude protein g/kg	Crude protein in ration kg	MJDE per kg	MJDE fed
Average hay	8.00	75	0.600	8	64
Naked oats	7.40	112	0.784	15	105
Alfalfa chaff	0.85	150	0.127	9	7.65
Totals	**(A) 16.25**		**(B) 1.51**		**~177**

To calculate the percentage protein in the ration (B) needs to be shown as a percentage of (A):

Thus B x 100, i.e. $\frac{1.51 \times 100}{16.25}$ = 9.3% protein in ration.

Although the above ration produces 2 MJDE per day more than the calculation showed necessary (175 required, 177 fed), the energy content of all the above may vary depending on the quality of the feed.

While this feed plan fulfils all dietary requirements in respect of crude protein and digestible energy it does, however, have nutritional shortcomings:

- The high proportion of oats results in a very poor calcium to phosphorus ratio, lysine and methionine deficiency and insufficient fibre.
- Oats should not make up more than 90 per cent of the concentrate ration.

Therefore a supplement of vitamins, minerals (in particular calcium), amino acids and salt would be needed daily. Alfalfa could also be used as an alternative to chaff, which would help redress the calcium to phosphorus issue and its higher energy and protein content per kilogram would allow a further reduction in the intake of oats. A further alternative to feeding oats would be to use a competition coarse mix as shown in the next example based upon the following tabular extract:

	Weight fed per day kg	Crude protein g/kg	Crude protein in ration kg	MJDE per kg	MJDE fed
Average hay	8.0	75	0.60	8.0	64
Competition coarse mix	7.0	120	0.84	12.5	84
Alfalfa chaff	1.0	150	0.15	9.0	9
Soya oil	0.25	0	0	35.0	8.75
Totals	**16.25**		**1.59**		**~166**

In this case, the protein element will be: $\dfrac{1.59 \times 100}{16.25} = 9.8\%$ protein in the ration.

This feed plan provides 9.8 per cent protein but is 9 MJDE short (175 required, 166 fed). However, the nutritional balance of vitamins, minerals and amino acids would be excellent as the coarse mix would provide a total balance and the soya oil has been used to increase the energy density of the ration without increasing protein intake.

It can be seen that the types of concentrates needed in rations are influenced by the quality of the hay, and the situation is complicated further when the horse has access to grazing, since both the quantity available and its quality will change throughout the year. However, these complications are not a reason for avoiding turning out.

In the next example we shall use good quality hay for the same horse:

	Weight fed per day kg	Crude protein g/kg	Crude protein in ration kg	MJDE per kg	MJDE fed
Good hay	8.0	100	0.80	10	80
Competition coarse mix	7.0	120	0.84	12	84
Alfalfa chaff	1.0	150	0.15	9.0	9
Soya oil	0.25	0.0	0.0	35.0	8.75
Totals	**16.25**		**1.79**		**~182**

In this example, there is $\dfrac{1.79 \times 100}{16.2} = 11\%$ protein in the ration.

This ration provides a little over the required level of MJDE per day and the percentage of protein provided is rather too high. This could be amended by replacing the alfalfa chaff with a hay, oat straw or alfalfa/oat straw mix and by reducing the quantity of soya oil fed.

Alternatively, a concentrate feed containing a lower percentage of protein could be used to substitute some of the competition coarse mix.

ITQ 99
a. Can you suggest some suitable alternative concentrates for the ration just mentioned?
b. List the five points that you need to know before being able to calculate a ration.

ITQ 100 Having calculated the above correctly, what other factors must be taken into account?

The 'Non-Scientific' Method of Calculating Feed Rations

Next, we will look at a less technical method of calculating rations. The quantities are based on the previous calculations and have been summarized in table format for ease of reference.

Useful measurements:

1 kg = 2.2 lb

1 lb = 0.45 kg

An average section of hay weighs approximately 1.8 kg (4 lb)

When filled level, a normal 1500 ml (2½ pint) feed scoop holds the following:

    1.35 kg (3 lb) cubes

    0.56 kg (1¼ lb) flaked barley

    1.35 kg (3 lb) soaked sugar beet pulp

    0.33 kg (0.75 lb) chaff

    0.67 kg (1½ lb) coarse mix

    1.35 kg (3 lb) carrots

    0.45 kg (1 lb) bran

Maximum daily requirements calculated upon horse's weight:

Height hh	Approx. weight kg	x 2.5% bw		Daily food kg	Equivalent lb
12	250	x 2.5%	=	6.25	13.75
13	300	x 2.5%	=	7.50	16.50
14	400	x 2.5%	=	10.00	22.00
15	450	x 2.5%	=	11.25	24.75
16	575	x 2.5%	=	14.40	31.70
17	650	x 2.5%	=	16.25	36.00

The table below shows the approximate daily feed for a horse in light work, based on a forage to concentrates ratio of 60:40. (Amounts shown allow for adjustments to be made. Also, when calculating feed rations, round amounts up or down to the nearest half kg or lb – do not complicate matters by dealing with small fractions.)

hh	Approx. daily amount		60% Forage		40% Concentrates	
	kg	lb	kg	lb	kg	lb
12	5.4–6.3	12–14	3.4–3.8	7.5–8.5	2.0–2.5	4.5–5.5
13	6.3–7.2	14–16	3.8–4.3	8.5–9.5	2.5–2.9	5.5–6.5
14	8.1–9.9	18–22	5.0–5.8	11.0–13.0	3.1–4.0	7.0–9.0
15	9.9–11.25	22–25	5.8–6.75	13.0–15.0	4.0–4.5	9.0–10.0
16	12.6–14.4	28–32	7.6–8.5	17.0–19.0	5.0–5.8	11.0–13.0
17	14.4–16.2	32–36	8.5–9.6	19.0–21.5	5.8–6.5	13.0–14.5

SAMPLE FEED CHARTS

The following feed charts have been devised for horses and ponies turned out all day on average grazing and stabled at night. They are in light work, competing in Riding/Pony Club events at weekends. Assume that they are all around eight years old, of calm disposition and maintain condition well.

There are many types of feedstuffs to choose from – while those used in the following sample rations are suitable there may be other similar feeds which are equally suitable.

All weights shown are *dry weights* but, while many feeds may be fed dry, it improves mastication and aids digestion if the feeds are well dampened. Many owners like to feed sugar beet pulp as it dampens the feed, provides a non-heating energy source, keeps weight on and is suitable for all horses and ponies. Boiled barley and linseed may also be given occasionally, especially after hard work or to improve condition.

When calculating the ration to include sugar beet or boiled barley or linseed, weigh the beet, barley or linseed *dry* and reduce one of the other feedstuffs by the same amount. Do not take into account the weight of the water in which the pulp, barley or linseed has been soaked or cooked, as the water does not contain the nutrients – these are derived from the dry feed.

Care should be taken when adding straight feeding stuffs to a compound mix or cube as this can unbalance the ration. Addition of cereals to a mix or cube can reduce the overall calcium to phosphorus ratio. Furthermore, the addition of other components such as sugar beet or chaff, and the subsequent adjustment of other constituents may reduce the quantities of the mix or cube below what is needed to maintain condition. In this situation an additional vitamin and mineral supplement may be necessary, or alternatively a feed balancer may be more appropriate.

Please note that these charts are working examples, originally based on imperial weights. The conversions to metric weight are approximations to a maximum of two decimal places, which causes some minor anomalies when the metric weights are totalled.

13 hh pony	kg	lb
Hay	4.54	10
Concentrates	2.72	6
Daily total	**7.26**	**16**

Morning feed			Evening feed		
kg	lb		kg	lb	
1.13	2.5	Horse & pony cubes	1.13	2.5	Horse & pony cubes
0.23	0.5	Chaff	0.23	0.5	Chaff
1.81	4	Hay	2.72	6	Hay
3.17	**7**		**4.08**	**9**	

14 hh pony	kg	lb
Hay	5.90	13
Concentrates	3.63	8
Daily total	**9.53**	**21**

Morning feed			Evening feed		
kg	lb		kg	lb	
1.36	3	Horse & pony cubes	1.36	3	Horse & pony cubes
0.23	0.5	Chaff	0.23	0.5	Chaff
0.23	0.5	Sugar beet	0.23	0.5	Sugar beet
1.81	4	Hay	4.10	9	Hay
3.63	**8**		**5.92**	**13**	

15 hh horse	kg	lb
Hay	6.35	14
Concentrates	4.54	10
Daily total	**10.89**	**24**

Morning feed			Evening feed		
kg	lb		kg	lb	
0.23	0.5	Chaff	0.23	0.5	Chaff
1.59	3.5	Coarse mix	1.59	3.5	Coarse mix
1.81	4	Hay	0.45	1	Carrots
			5.00	11	Hay
3.63	**8**		**7.27**	**16**	

16 hh horse	kg	lb
Hay	7.26	16
Concentrates	7.26	16
Daily total	**14.52**	**32**

This horse is stabled most of the time, turned out for three hours daily. He is being fittened for showjumping and Novice Horse Trials, has a slightly 'fizzy' nature and is prone to losing condition.

Morning feed			Lunchtime feed			Evening feed		
kg	lb		kg	lb		kg	lb	
0.45	1	Alfalfa chaff	1.81	4	Non-heating coarse mix	0.45	1	Alfalfa chaff
1.81	4	Non-heating coarse mix	1.81	4	Hay	1.81	4	Non-heating coarse mix
1.81	4	Hay	0.45	1	Carrots	3.63	8	Hay
			0.45	1	Alfalfa chaff			
4.07	**9**		**4.52**	**10**		**5.89**	**13**	

127

17 hh Hunter Chaser	kg	lb
Hay	8.16	18
Concentrates	8.16	18
Daily total	**16.32**	**36**

Racing regularly, working at least 1–2 hours daily to keep fit; six years old, steady temperament.

Morning feed			Lunchtime feed			Evening feed		
kg	lb		kg	lb		kg	lb	
0.45	1	Alfalfa chaff	0.45	1	Alfalfa chaff	0.45	1	Alfalfa chaff
2.04	4.5	Oats	2.04	4.5	Oats	2.04	4.5	Oats
0.23	0.5	Oat balancer	0.23	0.5	Oat balancer	0.23	0.5	Oat balancer
1.36	3	Hay	1.36	3	Hay	5.44	12	Hay
4.08	**9**		**4.08**	**9**		**8.16**	**18**	

ITQ 101 Approximately how much by weight does a level 1500 ml (2½ pint) scoop hold of the following feedstuffs?

                          Kg   Lb

a. Cubes –

b. Flaked barley –

c. Chaff –

d. Coarse mix –

e. Bran –

SUMMARY OF CRITERIA FOR RATIONING

The following factors will all affect what and how much a horse will be fed:

- Time of year – how much feed value is there in the grass?
- Whether turned out or stabled.

- Work – hacking, eventing, showjumping, dressage, hunting, racing, endurance, polo?
- Ability to maintain condition; metabolic efficiency.
- Temperament – calm or 'fizzy'?
- Type – cobby or Thoroughbred? Light, medium or heavyweight?
- Age – very young or old?
- Susceptibility to conditions such as exertional rhabdomyolsis (azoturia), laminitis.
- Allergies.
- Pregnancy and lactation.

> ITQ 102 Why do you need to know how much the horse weighs when calculating a feed ration?

MONITORING CONDITION

Although feed values can be calculated mathematically and scientifically, there can never be a substitute for good old-fashioned common sense, bearing in mind the saying 'the eye of the master maketh the horse'. The majority of horse owners feed through a 'feel' of what is right for their particular horse. By combining a few common sense points with the science of feeding, one can be assured of a well-fed horse.

1. **Always keep an eye on the condition of the horse**

   Is he losing weight or putting on too much? What condition do you want him in? For example, is he a show hunter or eventer? The show hunter will be required to carry more condition while the eventer should be free of superfluous fat. Increase or decrease feedstuffs accordingly.

   The horse should appear well covered but not 'flabby'. When viewed from behind the spine should appear to be level with the muscle of the hindquarters. If it projects prominently above the muscle, the horse is not carrying enough condition. If it appears sunken below the line of the muscle, the horse is overweight. The overweight horse will have heavy pads of fat on the crest, shoulders, barrel and hindquarters. The belly may also be too large, giving the impression that the horse is in foal.

   The thin horse will show his ribs, hips and spine prominently, with sunken areas where the muscle should be.

2. **Temperamentally, is he a 'hothead' or a calm, unflappable type?**

   This will help you to decide the most appropriate mix of fibre and starch-based concentrate feeds. Many 'fizzy' horses event successfully on a high-fibre diet supplemented with oil.

3. **Does he seem to have too much or too little energy for the job required?**

A Riding Club dressage horse will not need to be as energetic as an eventer. If the horse is too energetic and/or his behaviour deteriorates, the feedstuffs containing high starch levels may have to be replaced with others that are higher in fibre and lower in energy density.

However, if the horse feels lethargic and lacking in enthusiasm for work, provided that he is not overweight he may need to have the starch-based feedstuffs in his ration increased. *All changes should be made gradually, to avoid digestive disturbances.* Metabolic disorders such as laminitis and azoturia may result if carbohydrates are increased by too much, too quickly.

4. **Environmental conditions will affect feed intake**

In cold weather the horse will need warming feeds. Hay is ideal as its slow energy release produces an excellent source of energy and body heat. In the spring and summer he may be out at grass, so feed rations may be reduced if the grass is of good quality.

5. **Adjust rations according to the horse's appetite**

Always make sure that he enjoys his food. Some horses are naturally good doers while others tend to be poor. Feed to slightly below appetite, especially if the horse doesn't clear up all of his food. The horse will cope best with more, smaller feeds.

Check the teeth for sharp edges, which may affect the ability to chew. Some fit competition horses go off their food during training. They may need variety or simply a rest from large quantities of energy feeds.

6. **Worm regularly**

No amount of high quality food will keep a horse in good condition if he is suffering from a parasitic burden. Adhere to a regular worming programme.

COSTINGS

The monthly feed bill is a major expense to both the private horse owner and yard manager. The cost of feeding needs to be calculated and comparisons made to ensure that you are using the most cost-effective, good quality feedstuffs. Costs will vary from one manufacturer to another – you need to take into account preferences (both yours and the horses'), as well as cost when choosing between the different brands of horse feeds.

Another comparison to be made is that between the cost of feeding straights compared to compounds. Once you know exactly how much food each horse receives each day, it is easy to calculate.

If you are running a yard of several horses it is worth approaching the manufacturers direct, to negotiate buying wholesale in bulk. This will reduce the cost per kilogram – although you will be presented with a larger one-off invoice to pay. If buying in bulk you must also consider:

- **Shelf life**. Check the expiry dates and be sure to use before them.

- **Storage**. Ensure that your storage area is vermin-free and dry to prevent wastage. Bulk deliveries are often palleted, i.e. sacks on pallets. Do you have suitable access and, if necessary, the means of unloading (fork lift)?

- **Re-stocking**. Re-order in plenty of time and bring old stock to the front to be used first.

It is a more accurate method of purchase to pay for hay by the tonne (metric 1000 kg) rather than by the bale. However, it is frequently sold 'by the bale' so you must be sure to check the quality and weight of the average bale in your load. The amount of hay in a bale can vary tremendously – some bales are so light they can be picked up in one hand and carried by a small stable girl, whereas others are so heavy you can barely move them! At least you know if you buy by the tonne – a tonne of hay is a tonne of hay regardless of how many bales there are.

CHAPTER SUMMARY

The main aim of this chapter was to explain how rations are calculated and formulated. As a result of the work carried out by equine nutritionists, we now have a greater understanding of the nutritional needs of the horse; these needs can be met through correct ration formulation. Although the process appears complicated, the wide range of specially prepared cubes and mixes has simplified the calculations.

While it is essential to learn the theory of equine nutrition, it has to be put to the test in the day-to-day feeding of a variety of horses – continual monitoring and assessment of condition and performance will prove whether your rations are effective or not. All horses are different in the way in which they metabolize their food – they may not respond to a particular diet in the way you would expect. Remember that the horses don't read the same books as us!

Each horse has to treated as an individual. If the horses in your care are regularly wormed, look well and have enough energy for their given spheres without being 'over the top', then you are doing a good job!

CHAPTER 7

PHYSIOLOGICAL ADAPTATIONS TO TRAINING

The aims and objectives of this chapter are to explain:

- Why horses need to be fittened.
- The general aim of fittening horses.
- How to assess the horse's level of fitness through observation of muscle development, physical condition, skin health, weight and temperament at rest.
- How to assess the horse's level of fitness during and after exercise.
- The ways in which the respiratory, circulatory, muscular and skeletal systems respond and adapt to training.
- The mechanics of locomotory respiratory coupling.
- The anatomical changes that occur during exercise.
- The signs and causes of fatigue.
- The horse's thermoregulatory system.
- The causes, signs and treatment of dehydration.
- The causes, signs and treatment of heat stroke.

First we need to understand why horses need to be fittened.

WHY HORSES NEED TO BE FITTENED

There are two basic, inter-related reasons why it is necessary to get a horse fit for the task in hand – the first is ethical consideration for the horse's welfare and the second is the practical consideration that he should be capable of doing what is required in good form and without undue risk. In Chapter 2 we discussed the 'five freedoms' – the criteria against which horse management systems should be appraised. When discussing the five freedoms in relation to equine welfare, the lot of the competition horse is frequently overlooked. Most top-class competition horses are very valuable, live in five-star accommodation, have all the best tack and equipment and are treated extremely well. Well-managed competition horses also spend time turned out to grass.

However, competition brings about it own welfare issues, at all levels and in various respects. If horses are not trained to the appropriate level, are not fit enough and are unused to the climate or conditions in which they are competing, they are likely to experience physical and thermal discomfort, possibly fear, almost certainly distress and in a worst case scenario, injury and pain. Therefore, attention to fitness and thorough preparation are essential elements of equine management. A horse fit and prepared for his particular discipline will be able to participate without undue stress and fatigue. This applies to the respiratory system, the circulatory system and the muscles, tendons and ligaments.

If a horse is worked beyond his level of fitness, his health and soundness will be compromised in respect of the following:

Heart. Heart muscle responds to fitness work – the heart becomes stronger and more efficient. If overstretched, the heart will have to work much harder, beyond its limitations, which could, in certain cases, lead to death.

Muscles. If the under-developed respiratory and circulatory systems are not supplying the muscles with sufficient oxygen the tissues become **acidotic**, which can lead to exertional rhabdomyolysis (azoturia).

Tendon injury. If the muscles are fatigued, extra strain is borne by the tendons of the lower leg, which increases the risk of tendon injury.

Fatigue related injury. A tired horse is at increased risk of becoming injured by hitting a fence, falling or striking into himself as he gallops.

The general aim of fittening a horse is, therefore, to enable him to participate in a given discipline with minimum fatigue and risk of injury. He should be able to work for longer before fatigue occurs, and compete without distress. The requirements for each discipline will vary, for example an Advanced dressage horse must be supremely supple and very fit but, because of the different stresses placed on the various systems of the horse, he would not necessarily be fit to compete in say, a point-to-point.

The fitness level for any particular discipline is achieved through regular exercise over a period of time. It should be noted, however, that all horses, whether competing or not, require exercise.

In the wild, horses spend their days roaming, exercising themselves freely, resting as and when they desire. Similarly, a grass-kept horse will exercise himself in the field – although this will not be sufficient to achieve and maintain fitness for competition and/or hunting.

Daily exercise is needed for the following reasons:

- Exercise promotes the circulation of body fluids within the cardiovascular and lymphatic systems, thereby aiding their effective functioning. This circulation also promotes effective digestion and the removal of waste products (some waste products being excreted via the skin when the horse sweats).

- The respiratory system is developed, so promoting an improved supply of oxygen to the muscles.

- The muscles respond to the stimulation of schooling and exercise, becoming supple and well developed.

- The horse will become mentally relaxed – horses who are under-exercised often have a tendency to be 'uptight' and difficult to handle.

ASSESSMENT OF FITNESS LEVELS

Before you can begin to plan your fitness programme, you need to know the horse's present stage of fitness. Obviously, if he is your horse, or the horse has been in your care for some time, you'll know what work he's been doing. However, certain situations arise when you need to assess a horse's level of fitness without prior knowledge of him. Examples include:

- Before purchasing a horse – you need to know how fit the horse is and the effect this has on his behaviour, temperament, musculature and general condition.

- After purchasing a horse, especially if he has come from the sales. A private vendor or dealer *should* give you honest information about the horse and his fitness.

- A new livery arriving at your yard.

- During a practical examination.

- If advising a pupil of their horse's fitness and ability to compete in a specific event.

WORK TYPES AND FITNESS LEVELS

Before carrying out any assessment of fitness you need to know 'fit for what?' A horse could be perfectly fit enough to go unaffiliated showjumping but not fit enough to go hunting or eventing. The following list of work types is set out in an approximate ascending scale of fitness:

Lowest level of fitness
{
Light hacking and schooling.
Non-jumping showing classes.
Showing classes involving jumping
(such as Working Hunter).
Riding club dressage competition.
Riding club showjumping competition.
Showjumping up to Foxhunter level.

Hunter trials.

Riding Club one-day events.

Showjumping up to Grade A.

32 km (20 mile) long-distance rides.

BE one-day events – Novice.

Advanced dressage competition.

Hunting three times a fortnight.

BE one-day events – Intermediate to Advanced.

BE two-day events – Novice, Intermediate.

Highest level of fitness $\begin{cases} \text{BE/FEI three-day events – Novice,} \\ \text{Intermediate, Advanced.} \\ \text{Flat racing.} \\ \text{Point-to-pointing and National Hunt racing.} \end{cases}$

ITQ 103 What is the general aim of fittening?

ITQ 104 List four reasons why horses need exercise.

ASSESSMENT OF FITNESS AT REST

Observation of the horse at rest can give indications of his fitness status. When looking at a horse for the first time to assess fitness, there are certain features to consider:

1. **How old is the horse?** If he is very young (four or younger) or very old (eighteen or over), it is unlikely that he will be particularly fit. An exception to this would be in the case of a fittened two-year-old Thoroughbred being prepared for the racetrack. Also, some veteran horses compete and hunt – take this into account.

2. **Is he shod?** The majority of horses need to be shod when in work. An unshod horse is unlikely to have been in work.

3. **Is he clipped and trimmed?** In winter the horse would need to have been clipped to carry out a medium workload. If the horse is clipped and fully trimmed it gives a clue that he has *probably* been in work.

Having taken the above points into account you can look more specifically at his physical condition, muscular development and heart rate. The charts that follow will help in assessing these factors.

Physical condition	
Unfit and/or unwell	**Fit and well**
Overweight. The horse may be fit enough to compete in a showing class but will not be event fit.	The horse is free of excess fat yet carrying condition (score 2–3).
Underweight. Some horses 'run up light' when fit, especially after strenuous exercise – this mustn't be confused with being underweight.	You should be able to feel the ribs when you run your fingers across them but they should not be visibly obvious.
Coat dull and staring. Horse may be suffering from a nutrient deficiency or worm burden.	The coat should be glossy.
Skin dry and taut. The horse may be suffering from a nutrient deficiency or be dehydrated.	Skin should be supple and relatively loose.
Nasal discharge and/or **coughing**. Horse may be suffering from a respiratory tract infection or have a dust allergy.	Horse should be free of nasal discharge and coughs.
Dull attitude. If the horse shows a lack of interest in surroundings and goings-on he may be suffering from an ailment, e.g. a virus.	The horse should be interested in his surroundings, seeming bright and alert.

Muscle tone and development	
Unfit	**Fit**
Lack of muscle tone. The muscles of the neck, shoulders and hindquarters will appear soft, flaccid and undeveloped. Because of the lack of developed muscle there will either be hollows or pads of fat, dependent upon the horse's condition.	**Good muscular development.** The muscles of the neck, shoulders and hindquarters feel firm and well-developed. **Good muscle tone.** Look for increased muscle tone (taut and free of excess flesh) to help you decide if he has run up light or is simply too thin. The horse may have 'run up light', especially if he has just competed in a demanding discipline, e.g. a three-day event.

Figure 21 Areas of muscle development

Resting heart rate*	
Unfit	**Fit**
The normal parameters are between 25–40 beats per minute.	The resting heart rate may be relatively low – may be as low as 26 beats per minute. Standing under tack the heart rate will be between 40–65 beats per minute.
An elevated heart rate at rest could be indicative of pain.	The heart rate should be regular – however, dropped or skipped beats are common in well-conditioned horses at rest.

*It is necessary to appreciate that the resting heart rate of each individual will vary from horse to horse. For rates to be of value, it is necessary to know the horse's normal rates.

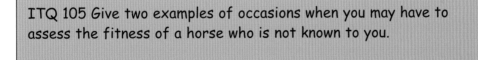

ITQ 105 Give two examples of occasions when you may have to assess the fitness of a horse who is not known to you.

ASSESSMENT OF FITNESS AFTER EXERCISE

Having made an initial assessment at rest, it will be necessary to work the horse to gain an accurate indication of his fitness. Begin by working the horse in walk and trot. If he copes easily with normal trot work, i.e. he does not become very out of breath, work him in properly and then do some canter work. Start off with a steady canter as it could be detrimental to an unfit horse to be worked at speed.

As with the trot, if he copes easily with 2 minutes of a normal working canter, build it up to a stronger pace. Gauge his breathing and heart rate before building up the work. The fitter he is, the more work it will take to increase his heart rate and the quicker he will recover. Again, the information given in the charts that follow will help your assessment.

Respiration and Exercise	
Unfit	**Fit**
Noisy breathing – may sound 'wet'.	The breathing will sound relaxed and regular.
Coughing – may be persistent and wet-sounding. Occurs as accumulated mucus from the lungs is cleared or may be the result of respiratory disease.	The horse should not cough. Some horses will always cough once or twice when first out, but should do no more.
Respiratory rate increases after gentle exercise. Normal 'at rest' rates are 8–16 breaths per minute.	Gentle exercise does not cause a significant increase in respiratory rate.
The horse may appear 'out of breath', i.e. he will blow after slightly more strenuous exercise. If very unfit he may appear distressed.	Slightly strenuous exercise causes only a slight increase and the rates return to base rate quickly.
After more strenuous exercise the horse takes longer than 10 minutes to recover from his working respiratory rates to his base rate.	Strenuous exercise causes the horse to 'blow' but he returns to base rate in less than 10 minutes.

Heart Rate and Exercise	
(The parameters for normal heart rates in the fit horse are shown in Table 11)	
Unfit	**Fit**
The heart rate will increase above the levels shown in Table 11 below. After strenuous exercise it takes 30 minutes or longer for the heart rate to reach 68 bpm or below. If, after 30 minutes the heart rate is above 68 bpm, the horse is very unfit and probably distressed.	After strenuous exercise the heart rate will be below 68 bpm within 10 minutes.

Activity	Heart rate (beats per minute)
Rest	30–40
Standing under tack	40–65
Walking	60–80
Slow trot	90–110
Fast trot	140–160
Canter	120–170
Gallop	160–200
Maximum/race speeds	205–240

Table 11 Approximate heart rates

Sweating	
Unfit	**Fit**
The horse may sweat after gentle exercise. Take into account the climate – on a very hot day all horses will sweat more regardless of their level of fitness. Also, an unclipped winter coat will cause the horse to sweat more.	If clipped and working in normal, i.e. not excessively hot conditions, the horse will not sweat heavily during moderate exercise. After prolonged, strenuous exercise the horse will sweat as a means of cooling down.
The sweat of an unfit horse is likely to be of a thick, white lather. This is caused by a build-up of proteins in the sweat glands which encourages the sweat to spread over a greater surface area, thus facilitating effective cooling. The unfit horse will, through lack of work, have sweated infrequently, resulting in a build-up of these sweat proteins.	The sweat of a fittened horse will be clearer, with less white lather. As mentioned above, regular sweating from exertion, i.e. the fittening regime, will deplete the level of proteins within the sweat glands, resulting in less lather.
The unfit horse will produce more heat than a fittened one as his circulatory and muscular systems are not conditioned and will therefore have to work harder than a fit horse to produce the same amount of energy.	Less heat is produced by the fittened horse as his muscle fibres are conditioned. Capillarization (increase in capillaries serving the muscles) increases the amount of oxygen carried to the muscles, promoting efficient tissue respiration (energy production) and thus reducing the amount of heat produced.

ITQ 106 What might cause an elevated resting heart rate in the horse?

ITQ 107 What are the normal parameters for the horse's heart rates when:

a. Standing under tack?

b. Walking?

c. Trotting strongly?

d. Cantering?

e. Galloping?

SOUNDNESS

Another aspect to be considered when assessing fitness is that of soundness – you will not be able to fitten a horse if there is a question about his soundness. Whatever the level of competition the horse is being fittened for, he has to start his fitness programme one hundred per cent sound and stay sound through to the end of the season, if he is to continue to compete.

Regarding soundness of limbs, the horse's lower legs should be free from heat, puffiness and swellings. The legs should feel cold with clean, well-defined tendons. In all gaits the horse should not show any deviation from a normal stride. The steps should be regular and even – any shortening or unevenness indicates an underlying problem. Many soundness problems can be avoided by careful preparation and fittening, and through adequate leg protection, i.e. boots and/or bandages being used when working, especially when jumping.

However, horses' legs are put under ever-increasing stress throughout their competitive career and there are times when, regardless of the precautions taken, things go wrong and the horse becomes unsound. If this happens, he must be taken out of work, the problem resolved, and returned to fitness before attempting to compete again.

Although the term 'soundness' is most commonly used with reference to the limbs, it actually encompasses much more than this. Fitness training brings about physiological adaptations to the circulatory, muscular and skeletal systems. These changes (which, at a deeper level, also impact on the limbs themselves) allow the horse to function with greater efficiency, enabling him to perform at a higher level of intensity. We will now look at the effect that fittening work has on these systems.

ADAPTATIONS TO TRAINING

THE RESPIRATORY SYSTEM

The normal rate of breaths per minute in the adult horse at rest is between 8 and 16. Youngstock have a slightly higher rate. During strenuous exercise the rate may increase to 120 breaths per minute in order to cope with the body's extra oxygen requirements.

One aim of fitness work with any horse is to increase his ability to supply and utilize oxygen. Aerobic capacity improves as a result of adaptations made by the horse's cardiovascular system and changes within the muscle fibres. These are discussed later in this chapter. Research has shown that the equine respiratory system itself does not respond to training.

As the horse's general fitness improves, so his muscles will develop. This development gives a number of advantages (see The Muscular System, later this chapter) but, with respect to basic respiration, the developing muscles will include those of the diaphragm and chest, further aiding efficient breathing. (The internal and external abdominal oblique and the internal intercostal muscles are the primary expiratory muscles. The diaphragm and external intercostal muscles are involved in inspiration.)

Thus, the main adaptations that occur within the respiratory system are:

- Pulmonary capillarization – the proliferation of the capillaries supplying the alveolar sacs increases the area over which gaseous exchange can take place.
- Improved development of the muscles involved in respiration, thereby aiding the physical mechanics of respiration.

We will now look at the mechanics of the respiratory system during exercise.

Locomotory Respiratory Coupling

At canter and gallop, the respiratory rate is locked to the stride rate. This synchronicity is a mechanical advantage known as **locomotory respiratory coupling**. The synchrony between the stride frequency and respiratory rate ensure that locomotion doesn't interfere with ventilation and the uptake of oxygen.

At canter and gallop the respiratory rate and stride frequency are linked in a 1:1 ratio. This will mean that the maximum respiratory rate equals 150 breaths per minute because the maximum number of strides a horse can achieve is approximately 150 per minute.

As the horse gallops, there is a moment of suspension when the head is raised, causing the thoracic muscles to pull the rib cage forwards. Also, the internal viscera (internal organs) are pushed back. The combination of pulling the rib cage forwards and decompressing the internal organs allows more air to the lungs upon inhalation. This is known as the **thoracic unloading phase**.

On landing after the moment of suspension, the head is lowered and the internal organs move forward, acting as an internal piston compressing the lungs and forcing air out, causing exhalation. This is known as the **thoracic loading phase**.

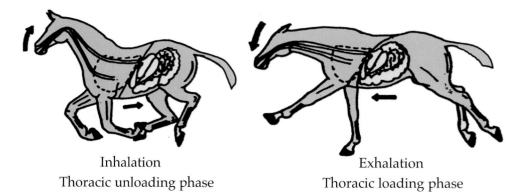

Inhalation
Thoracic unloading phase

Exhalation
Thoracic loading phase

Figure 22 Locomotory respiratory coupling

Anatomical Changes during Exercise

The respiratory tract is divided up into the upper respiratory tract (URT) and the lower respiratory tract (LRT).

During fast work, the URT shows changes which reduce resistance and facilitate inhalation and exhalation. These changes include:

- Dilation of the nostrils.

- Straightening of the respiratory tract.

- Dilation of the nasopharynx and larynx.

ITQ 108
a. Name the muscles involved in expiration.

b. Name the muscles involved in inspiration.

ITQ 109 What is meant by 'pulmonary capillarization'?

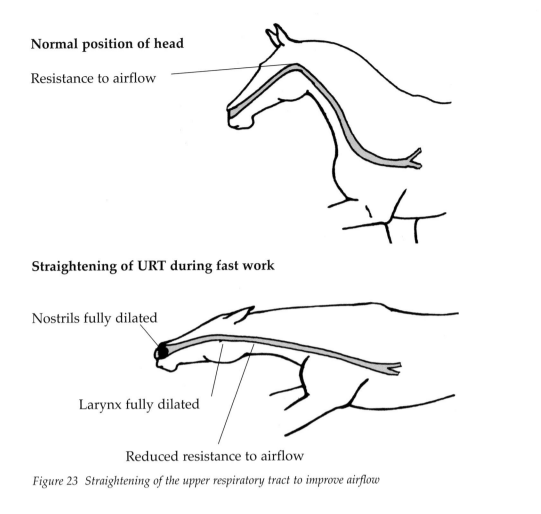

Normal position of head

Resistance to airflow

Straightening of URT during fast work

Nostrils fully dilated

Larynx fully dilated

Reduced resistance to airflow

Figure 23 Straightening of the upper respiratory tract to improve airflow

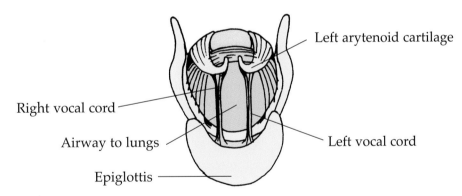

Left arytenoid cartilage

Right vocal cord

Airway to lungs

Left vocal cord

Epiglottis

The larynx during quiet breathing – vocal cords partially pulled aside

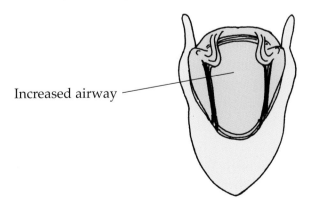

Increased airway

The larynx during fast work – vocal cords completely pulled aside

Figure 24 Dilation of the larynx

143

ITQ 110

a. During fast work, what is the horse's maximum respiratory rate?

b. Why is this the maximum rate?

ITQ 111 With reference to locomotory respiratory coupling, what is meant by the following?

a. The thoracic unloading phase.

b. The thoracic loading phase.

THE CIRCULATORY SYSTEM

Fitness work has a noticeable effect upon the circulatory system. As the duration and level of exercise increases, the muscles contract more often, resulting in the need for more oxygen and the removal of more waste products. As a response to the increase in demand for oxygen and removal of waste products, the capillary beds within the muscles proliferate and dilate, so increasing the volume of blood that flows through the capillary bed.

In order to cope with these extra demands, the circulatory system has to work efficiently. With work, the heart becomes increasingly efficient: the amount of blood pumped with each heartbeat (the **cardiac output**) increases. The heart also increases in size. The muscular ventricular wall may thicken and the ventricular chambers may become larger.

The blood also undergoes adaptations with training. These include an increase in the number of erythrocytes (red blood cells) and erythrocyte turnover, both of which increase the oxygen-carrying capacity of the blood and increased plasma volume. As well as facilitating the transport and removal of the waste products of metabolism, e.g. carbon dioxide and ammonia, increased plasma volume leads to improved efficiency of the horse's thermoregulation, as heat is dissipated in the blood.

A fit horse will:

- As a result of increased cardiac output, have a slower resting heart rate (may be as low as 26 beats per minute).

- Show a less marked increase in heart and respiratory rates after strenuous exercise.

- Recover after exercise more quickly, that is, respiratory and heart rates return to normal more quickly. (When the horse gallops, his heart rate may reach a maximum of 260 beats per minute.)

In an unfit horse, these adaptations are reversed.

During strenuous exercise, especially in an unfit horse, it is difficult for the body to provide enough oxygen for the muscle cells to cope with the workload. The muscles are forced to work anaerobically, resulting in lactic acid production. When lactic acid accumulates in the muscles, muscular fatigue and pain result. (Fatigue is discussed in greater detail later on in this chapter.) The oxygen debt is 'paid off' after the exercise and it is this that causes the respiratory rate to continue to be elevated when the horse is 'cooling-off'.

Thus, the main adaptations that occur within the circulatory system are:

- Capillary proliferation and dilation, which increases the transport of oxygen to the muscles during exercise.

- Improved heart efficiency, which results in increased cardiac output.

- Increased production and turnover of red blood cells, which increases the oxygen-carrying capacity of the blood.

- Improved thermoregulation as a result of increased plasma volume.

ITQ 112 What is meant by 'cardiac output'?

ITQ 113 Why does a fittened horse have a slower resting heart rate than an unfit one?

ITQ 114 List the main adaptations made by the circulatory system in response to fittening work.

ITQ 115 What is the main aim of these adaptations?

THE MUSCULAR SYSTEM

Increased muscular development is associated with improved fitness of the horse. This increased development occurs as a result of changes to the muscle fibres. These changes include:

- An increase in the activity of aerobic enzymes found within the **mitochondria** within the muscle fibres, resulting in an improved oxidative capacity of the muscle.

- Increase in capillarization, improving oxygen-carrying capacity and removal of waste products.

- Increased myoglobin, the muscle protein pigment which has the capacity for oxygen storage

(These changes aid oxygen availability and utilization, which in turn allows the muscle to function for longer.)

- Improved capacity to store glycogen – this means that more substrate is available to produce the energy required by the muscles. The onset of fatigue from energy depletion is then delayed and the horse is able to work for longer.

- Alterations to the fibre type within a muscle. Muscle fibre types are discussed in detail in Book 1 in this series, *Anatomy & Physiology*, however, they can be summarized thus:
  Slow-twitch fibres contract slowly and are known as **Type I fibres**. A horse with a high proportion of Type I fibres will be suited to endurance work rather than sprinting work. All slow-twitch fibres are high oxidative, which means they are very efficient at breaking down glycogen (**glycolytic**) and utilizing oxygen.
  Fast-twitch fibres are referred to as **Type II fibres** and are further divided into categories **A** and **B**.
  Type IIA fibres are fast-contracting, high oxidative/glycolytic fibres, which are versatile enough to provide power for both speed and endurance, thus they enable the horse to work for relatively long periods at relatively high speeds.
  Type IIB fibres are fast-contracting, low oxidative fibres, ideal for fast acceleration and sprinting, but they will become fatigued rapidly.
  Type IIB fibres decrease as Type IIA fibres increase.

THE SKELETAL SYSTEM

Bones are dynamic structures – they are continually changing and are able to adapt with fitness training. Exercise conditions the skeleton as bones respond to the stress of exercise by increasing in strength. Exercise and training cause more bone to be laid down by a process referred to as **remodelling**. Remodelling results in the formation of dense and stronger bone, which is able to withstand hard or fast work.

FATIGUE

Fatigue can be defined as the physiological inability to maintain a given activity or level of work. It is normally a temporary state, but there are certain conditions under which it may be prolonged.

SIGNS OF FATIGUE

The initial signs will be the obvious ones associated with a tired horse:

- Reluctance to continue at that level/speed, shown as slowing down and/or refusing to jump.
- The horses appears/feels tired and lacking in energy. This is sometimes described as being 'cooked', 'no petrol left in the tank', 'hitting the wall', etc.

Physiological signs of fatigue include:

- Elevated heart rate.
- High respiratory rate.
- Shallow respiration.
- Increased rectal temperature. (In fact, increased temperature overall, although commonly measured per rectum.)
- Depression and weakness.
- Reduced appetite and apparently reduced thirst. (Severe fatigue may cause the horse to be unwilling to drink, even though he may be dehydrated and needing to do so – see Dehydration later this chapter.)

CAUSES OF FATIGUE

The main reason why horses become fatigued is because their muscle function is impaired. This occurs in a selective manner, gradually reducing the performance of the horse.

Causes of muscle function impairment are:

- Glycogen depletion – depletion of the substrate for energy.
- Lactic acid (LA) accumulation – excess LA in the muscles produces cramps and pain.
- Electrolyte alteration – associated with dehydration.
- Increase in muscle temperature and reduced blood flow – a factor linked to heat stress (see Thermoregulation, this chapter).

Glycogen Depletion and Selective Recruitment of Muscle Fibres

Muscle cells contain a mosaic of all muscle fibre types and these are recruited selectively in accordance with the gait, speed and duration of exercise. To maintain posture and to exercise at very low levels, the fatigue-resistant slow-twitch (Type I) fibres are utilized. As the intensity of exercise increases, other fibre types begin to be recruited.

As the muscle fibres are brought into use the glycogen stores are progressively depleted. Without glycogen (the energy source) the horse will begin to become fatigued as muscle contractions weaken.

Lactic Acid Accumulation and Metabolic Acidosis

Almost all levels of activity involve a certain amount of anaerobic metabolism and consequently the production of lactic acid. As the work intensity increases, more fast-twitch low-oxidative (Type IIB) muscle fibres begin to be utilized and energy is produced by anaerobic respiration.

Lactic acid is then formed at a faster rate than it can be removed, resulting in a build-up of lactate in the muscles. Lactic acid in the muscles results in **acidosis**, which impairs muscle function. (Acidosis refers to the pH within the cells – the cells become acidotic, which impairs glycolysis and the respiratory capacity of the mitochondria.) Both of these are associated with reducing **ATP** (**adenosine triphosphate**) in the muscles and consequently with fatigue.

In extreme circumstances, acidosis may lead to the cramp-like condition **exertional rhabdomyolysis** (also known as azoturia/tying up).

> ITQ 116 List six physiological signs of fatigue.

> ITQ 117
> a. What causes glycogen depletion?
>
> b. What effect does this have on muscle function?

> ITQ 118
> a. What causes the production of lactate?
>
> b. What effect does an accumulation of lactate have on the muscles?

THERMOREGULATION

Energy required for muscle function is derived from the conversion of chemical energy (stored as glycogen or fat) to mechanical energy. This process is inefficient as it results in a loss of approximately 80% of energy as heat. Therefore the body temperature increases with exercise. However, the horse's body temperature must be maintained within a very narrow range and, for the body's core temperature to remain constant the excess heat must be dissipated. This is achieved through **thermoregulation**.

Thermoregulation describes the mechanism whereby heat is transferred from internal systems within the body to the environment, effectively cooling the horse. Cooling occurs by conduction, convection, radiation and evaporation if the horse's body temperature is higher than the ambient temperature and the humidity is not too high. Without these cooling mechanisms the body would overheat, with potentially fatal consequences (discussed later in this chapter).

TEMPERATURE RANGE IN THE HORSE

The normal rectal temperature of a horse is 38 °C (100.5 °F) but the core temperature is approximately 2 °C higher.

After activity, the temperature may rise to 39–39.4 °C (102–103 °F), which is not a cause for concern provided that the temperature doesn't remain static or increase further, or that the weather is not very hot or humid.

Temperatures of 40 °C (104 °F) and above indicate a critical level. If a temperature of 41 °C (105.8 °F) were maintained for any great length of time, the horse's life would be endangered. Temperatures as high as 42 °C (108 °F) and over are only seen in seriously ill horses. Tissue proteins actually break down in response to these high temperatures and thus, along with dehydration (see later this chapter), heat stress is potentially fatal. If left untreated, the horse will develop exertional rhabdomyolysis, ataxia (incoordination) and coma. Death usually follows.

REGULATION OF INTERNAL TEMPERATURE

The internal temperature is regulated by the **peripheral thermoreceptors**. These are temperature-sensitive nerve cells able to detect changes in temperature and elicit the appropriate physiological response. Peripheral thermoreceptors are located in the skin, skeletal muscle, abdomen, regions of the spinal cord and medulla oblongata (brain).

Mechanisms of Heat Loss

Heat is dissipated in three main ways in the horse:

1. **Cardiovascular changes**. The cardiovascular system responds to changes in the body temperature to help maintain a constant temperature. In hot conditions, blood flow is diverted from the internal body structures to the surface of the skin. Skin temperature then increases and heat is lost to the environment via conduction and radiation. The blood vessels near the skin dilate (**vasodilatation**), to increase blood flow to the surface. In cold conditions the opposite occurs, blood vessels constrict (**vasoconstriction**) to reduce heat loss from the blood.

2. **Respiratory losses**. This is an important mechanism in the horse. Inspired air is warmed as it passes through the upper respiratory tract. The warmed air is then expired, resulting in heat loss. In other animals this exchange takes the form of panting. In extreme conditions (when overheated), the horse may pant.

3. **Sweat evaporation.** This is the main means of heat loss and therefore maintenance of a stable body temperature. The conversion of fluid (sweat)

to vapour is an **endothermic** reaction, (a reaction requiring energy). Therefore the evaporation of sweat from the skin will take heat energy away from the body, thereby cooling the horse.

Sweating is only an efficient method of heat loss if the sweat evaporates. The amount of evaporation which takes place is dependent upon the environmental temperature and relative humidity. The hotter and more humid the climate, the less sweat will be evaporated, resulting in ineffective cooling.

We will now look at two problems associated with dysfunctions of thermoregulation which can prove, at best, performance-limiting and, at worst, life-threatening. These are dehydration and heat stroke.

> **ITQ 119**
> a. What is considered a normal rectal temperature after activity?
>
> b. What is considered a dangerous rectal temperature?

DEHYDRATION

Dehydration is a condition resulting from a loss of fluids and electrolytes from the body, which are not replaced.

CAUSES

In an otherwise healthy body, dehydration in the working horse generally occurs as a result of excessive sweating by a horse who does not receive enough to drink. This may occur when a horse is competing in hot, humid conditions. Even when not actually competing, horses at competition venues should be offered water very frequently (every 45 minutes; more frequently in hot weather and/or when the horse has sweated). This is particularly important with horses who tend not to drink readily at shows. In other situations, dehydration may result from poor management/neglect in the stable, the horse being left without water for several hours, or lack of water during transportation. Horses may sweat markedly during transit and even those who have not sweated should be offered water frequently (at least every $1^1/_2$ hours on a long journey, more frequently in hot weather or when the horse has sweated).

Effects and Consequences of Sweating

The exact amount of drinking water needed daily will depend on the size of the horse, combined with his work, diet and environmental conditions. The potential variation is substantial – somewhere between 18 and 76 litres (4–17 gallons).

Moderate to heavy sweating can result in a loss of approximately 5 litres (9 pints) of sweat each hour. A loss of 3 litres (5 pints) will result in a state of dehydration. Even in cool weather a horse may sweat between 6 and 8 litres ($10^1/_2$–14 pints) an hour if working at a steady canter. This will not cause problems if the humidity is low and the horse is given plenty to drink. A Thoroughbred racehorse can lose approximately 10 litres (17½ pints) in the warm-up and race over 2 miles.

The consequences of prolonged and/or heavy sweating are as follows. *A loss of:*

- 5 per cent of body fluids will result in mild dehydration
- 8 per cent leads to moderate dehydration
- 10 per cent is severe
- 12–15 per cent is life-threatening.

DISTRIBUTION OF BODILY FLUIDS

The average bodily water content of healthy horses is 70 per cent by weight.

Water is distributed in the body in a definite pattern, i.e. in two main compartments. These are:

Intracellular fluid (ICF) – the fluid within the body cells, comprising two-thirds of the total body water.

Extracellular fluid (ECF) – the fluid outside the body cells, comprising one third of the total body water. ECF is then further divided into:

Plasma water (PW) – the water within the blood vessels.

Interstitial fluid (ISF) – the water which fills the spaces between the cells.

FLUID AND ELECTROLYTE BALANCE

Normal metabolism and cellular functions can only continue in the presence of the correct balance of fluids and **electrolytes**. Electrolytes are substances that conduct electricity through their **ions**. Ions are atoms with either a positive electrical charge (a **cation**) or a negative electrical charge (an **anion**). There must be a balance between anions and cations to ensure electrical neutrality and therefore normal cell function.

The most important electrolytes in equine metabolism are sodium chloride (common salt), potassium, calcium, magnesium, phosphorus and the trace elements iron, copper, zinc, cobalt, selenium, sulphur and iodine. The presence of these electrolytes as constituents of bodily fluid varies according to the type of fluid.

The main cations in intracellular fluid are potassium and magnesium, with small amounts of sodium. Phosphorous is the major anion. Proteins, bicarbonate and sulphur are also present in intracellular fluid.

Plasma water contains sodium as the main cation, with smaller amounts of potassium, calcium and magnesium. The main anions are chloride and bicarbonate, with small amounts of phosphorous, sulphur, organic acids and proteins. Interstitial fluid contains everything found in plasma except the proteins.

> **ITQ 120** List three causes of dehydration in the otherwise healthy horse.

ITQ 121

a. How much fluid can be lost in an hour of moderate to heavy sweating?

b. In terms of fluid loss, how much will cause a state of mild dehydration?

ITQ 122

a. What is the average percentage of water in a horse in terms of bodyweight?

b. How is this fluid distributed within the body?

FLUID LOSS
Forms of Fluid Loss

There are two forms of fluid loss:

Primary water loss (true or pure dehydration) is caused when water intake is inadequate, normally because the horse cannot drink, e.g. as a result of neglect or a disease which causes difficulty in swallowing, such as tetanus. The water loss is shared by both body compartments, i.e. both ICF and ECF lose water.

Mixed water and electrolyte loss. Water and electrolytes are lost through excessive sweating. The loss of fluid and electrolytes through sweating has certain physiological effects:

- As fluid is drawn out of the blood vessels to form sweat, the blood volume becomes reduced.
- Thus blood viscosity increases.
- The oxygen-carrying capacity of the blood is reduced.
- The acid-base balance of the cells is disrupted.
- Cell function is impaired.
- The ability to sweat is reduced.
- Body temperature increases.

Consequences of Fluid Loss

The reduced blood flow leads to oxygen starvation within the tissues, causing the cells to switch to anaerobic metabolism. This leads to a build-up of lactic acid, which disrupts the pH levels in the cells.

Acidity is measured on the pH scale, which ranges from 1–14. A pH of 7 is 'neutral'. Solutions with a pH of less than 7 are **acids**; those with a pH greater than 7 are **alkalis** or **bases**. For cells to function normally, plasma must have a pH of 7.35–7.45. Any deviation from this will affect cellular and enzyme function. When the plasma pH falls, the cells become acidotic and normal function is impaired.

As the cooling system fails the horse may begin to pant heavily to lose heat via the lungs. In extreme cases a condition known as **synchronous diaphragmatic flutter (SDF)** or **'the thumps'** may develop. The diaphragm beats in rhythm with the heart, and this may be seen as unusual movement in the flank region. If severe, a thumping sound will also be heard. This condition is seen in horses suffering from a serious electrolyte imbalance and is caused by hypersensitivity of the phrenic nerve which supplies the diaphragm. At the point where this nerve passes over the heart, electrical activity stimulates it, causing the diaphragm to contract with each beat of the heart. This condition is treated by correcting the electrolyte imbalance.

SIGNS OF DEHYDRATION

- The horse appears dull and lethargic.
- Dry skin loses its pliability (See the skin pinch test, next section).
- Capillary and jugular refill times increase (See capillary and jugular refill tests, next section).
- Weight loss.
- Small, dry faeces.
- Decreased urine.
- Acidosis (blood becomes acidotic).
- Weakened pulse.
- As sweating stops the temperature rises and the conditions worsens.
- A thick, patchy sweat forms.
- The horse may pant.
- The eyeballs recede into their sockets.
- Mucous membranes initially become pale and tacky. As the dehydration worsens they become dry and purple-blue in colour.
- Gut sounds are reduced initially and may eventually stop completely.
- The horse may become disorientated, develop colic and go down.
- In extreme cases the horse may go into a coma before death occurs.

ITQ 123 What are the following?

a. Electrolyte.

b. Ion.

c. Cation.

d. Anion.

TESTING FOR DEHYDRATION

There are several tests that can be carried out to test for dehydration.

The skin pinch test. Dehydration causes a loss of skin elasticity – normally a pinch of skin from the neck would recoil to its usual position immediately. If the skin remains 'tented', taking longer than 2 seconds to recoil, the horse is dehydrated. The longer it takes to recoil, the more dehydrated the horse is. A recoil time of 4 seconds or more indicates serious dehydration.

The capillary refill test. Pressure on the horse's gum will press the blood out of the capillaries, causing the area to blanch. Normally the blanched area will return to pink as soon as the pressure is removed, as the blood flows back through the capillaries. If this takes 2 seconds or more, it indicates that the blood is too thick to circulate easily through the capillary network. A refill time of 4 seconds or more indicates a very serious (life-threatening) problem.

The jugular refill test. The blood can be squeezed from the jugular vein by running the thumb or forefinger down the jugular groove. When empty, feel the collapsed vein refill and become distended with blood. Normally this would happen immediately. If it takes longer than 2 seconds, this can be considered a warning sign. As with the other tests, a refill time of 4 seconds or more indicates a life-threatening degree of dehydration.

Haematology. The blood can be tested in various ways to determine the degree of dehydration.

- **The proportion of red blood cells to plasma** is measured as a percentage – this measurement is known as the **packed cell volume (PCV)**. The normal range of PCV is between 35 and 50 per cent – the average is 40 per cent. When a horse is dehydrated the PCV increases. A PCV of 55 per cent is very serious, 60 per cent + is grave, 65 per cent + is probably terminal.

- **Plasma proteins**. This reading is taken in conjunction with PCV at regular intervals to monitor the horse's progress.

- **Serum chloride levels**. If these are low it indicates electrolyte loss.

- **Blood pH and lactate levels**. This helps to ascertain the degree of acidosis.

TREATMENT OF DEHYDRATION

The main aim of treating dehydration is to replace the fluid lost and cool the horse as quickly as possible.

Fluid Replacement

In mild cases the horse must be encouraged to drink approximately 4.5 litres (1 gallon) of water every 15 minutes.

If the horse is accustomed to it, he may be offered an electrolyte solution. Electrolyte preparations are widely available and may be administered in the water or feed or given neat through a plastic syringe (orally). Note that electrolytes must only be given neat if the horse's stomach contains plenty of water. Neat electrolytes in an empty stomach will draw water from the blood vessels to absorb them.

The electrolyte solution in drinking water must not be too strong as that, too, will have an adverse effect, causing fluid to be drawn out of the blood supply to the gut and exacerbating the dehydration. The horse should always have plain water available too – not every horse will drink water containing electrolytes.

It is not possible to replace all of the elements lost in sweat in an electrolyte solution as the water would be too salty to drink. However, electrolytes can be added to the feed for several days before and after a strenuous event to compensate for losses. Some preparations contain glucose, dextrose or citrate to aid the absorption of the electrolytes.

In severe cases of dehydration the horse will need fluid therapy administered intravenously by the vet.

Cooling

The horse should be walked into a shaded area and sponged repeatedly with cold water to cool him down – cold water can be used on the large muscle masses provided the horse is kept walking to prevent him from tying up (exertional rhabdomyolysis). Heat is conducted from the skin to the water, which must then be scraped off immediately to aid cooling. If the water is not scraped off it heats up and acts as an insulator, keeping heat in.

In extreme heat and humidity, special precautions must be taken. A shaded area and cooling fans must be provided. Iced water can be used for washing off but, as mentioned, this must be scraped off immediately. The horse should be kept walking.

In severe cases, ice packs on the top of the head, down the neck and on the large blood vessels on the inside of the hind legs will help to cool the horse.

IN-TEXT ACTIVITY

Assuming that 70 per cent of his bodyweight is composed of water, calculate the approximate amount of water present in the body of a 10-year-old 500 kg horse.

a. Calculate 70 per cent of 500 kg.
b. Find out the weight of 1 litre of water.
c. Approximately how much water does this horse's body contain?
d. What fluid loss would cause this horse to suffer from moderate dehydration?

ITQ 124 What happens to the blood as a result of excessive sweating?

ITQ 125 Following changes to the blood, why do the cells start to respire anaerobically?

ITQ 126 What is the normal pH of plasma?

ITQ 127 What happens to the pH of the cells as a result of anaerobic respiration?

ITQ 128 Why, in hot conditions, does dehydration lead to overheating?

ITQ 129
a. By what other name is synchronous diaphragmatic flutter known?

b. Why is it so called?

ITQ 130 List five signs of dehydration.

IN-TEXT ACTIVITY

a. Perform the skin pinch and capillary and jugular refill tests on a healthy horse under normal conditions.

b. If you have the opportunity, for example, on a horse who has just returned from a day's hunting or who has just completed a speed and endurance type of competition (especially in hot conditions), do the same tests and compare your findings.

HEAT STROKE

As previously mentioned, the state of dehydration causes a fall in blood volume which adversely affects cooling – sweating is greatly reduced. If the body's cooling systems fail to lower the temperature to a safe level quickly, the horse will suffer from heat stress, also referred to as **heat stroke**.

Heat stroke usually affects dehydrated horses in the latter sections of endurance rides or on the cross-country phase of a horse trial in hot, humid conditions. A horse kept in a hot, ill-ventilated stable for many hours may also be affected.

The signs of heat stroke are:

- The core temperature increases – the rectal temperature will be high, 41.5–43.3 °C (106–110 °F).
- Depression and weakness.
- Elevated pulse and respiratory rate.
- The skin will feel hot and dry.
- The horse may stagger before going down.
- Coma followed by death.

Heat stroke must be treated very quickly under the advice of a vet. Before the vet reaches the horse, try to move him into the shade. Cool the horse as described in the treatment of dehydration.

CHAPTER SUMMARY

This chapter has introduced the general aims of fittening. We have looked at the ways in which the horse's initial level of fitness can be assessed, prior to the main fittening programme. To have an understanding of the general aims of fittening you need to know the effect fittening work has on the systems. We have therefore examined the physiological adaptations that occur.

Whilst fittening horses, you must be able to recognize the signs of fatigue. More importantly you need to know why horses become fatigued – what causes impaired muscle function. Moderate fatigue requires no specialist treatment – after an event a tired horse should have a rest day and be fed his usual rations, supplemented with electrolytes. He will recover quite naturally – his energy reserves will be restored with good feeding. However, fatigue can present a serious problem if complicated by dehydration and heat stress. As these conditions can be life-threatening they are of great significance. Competition horses, especially those competing in endurance and cross-country events in hot, humid climates, are at risk from these conditions. Prevention, where possible, is far preferable to treatment.

CHAPTER 8

FITTENING PROGRAMMES

The aims and objectives of this chapter are to explain:

- How to plan the type and duration of the fitness programme.
- The factors affecting the horse's ability to achieve fitness.
- The process of bringing the horse up from grass in preparation for work.
- The differences between the main types of fittening programmes.
- The terminology used in interval training.
- The use of additional training aids.

PLANNING THE FITNESS PROGRAMME

Before you can begin to plan your fitness programme you need to assess how fit you want the horse to be. The level of fitness needed must be judged as accurately as possible: to underestimate could result in an exhausted horse, with the possibility of a number of serious consequences.

However, there are no real benefits in having a horse over-fit, especially for the less demanding disciplines. If over-fit, horses tend to take longer to settle down at a competition venue, can be difficult to handle and need more work to maintain calmness.

When fittening horses, the overriding factor to be considered is that of *individuality*. Every horse is different and, depending upon temperament, age, record of soundness and the type of competition chosen, the fitness programme must suit each individual horse.

Experienced trainers have their own individual methods of working horses towards competition fitness. If you've trained many horses before you probably have your own tried and trusted method of fittening. However, as you read through this chapter, consider the comparisons between the methods described and the methods you use yourself.

FACTORS TO CONSIDER

When planning the programme, the following factors must be taken into account.

Time of year. If a horse has been out on lush grass and is overweight, he will take longer to get fit than if he had rested over the winter, rugged up, partially stabled and receiving short feeds.

Age. It is more difficult and potentially damaging to achieve full fitness of a very young horse, since youngsters are physically immature. Older horses may have problems associated with soundness.

Type and temperament. Generally, the keen, lighter, Thoroughbred type will be easier to get fit than a lazy, heavier sort.

Soundness. Any problem associated with soundness will result in much more time being needed, particularly with the early slow work.

Level of training. A horse who has already been fully fit once before will be easier to get fit again.

Type of competition. The type of competition will affect how fit the horse needs to be. It will take longer to get a horse fit for a three-day event than to get one ready for a Riding Club one-day event.

Key points:
- Assess the horse's current level of fitness.
- Decide how fit you need him to be.
- Find out when the first event is.

These are your starting points – you can then plan your fitness programme.

PREPARATION

Before starting to get a horse fit, checks should be made on the following points, and the appropriate action taken.

Feet. The horse must be shod, with stud holes if necessary.

Vaccinations. These must be given as protection against tetanus and equine influenza. Many competitive organizations demand proof of vaccination for equine influenza before allowing the horse to be registered. Even when this is not a requirement of the administrative body of your chosen discipline, it may be a requirement of individual show venues. Check closing/ballot dates for the first events and make sure that you allow enough time to get the horse vaccinated and registered.

Worming. A worm burden will prevent the horse from utilizing his food to maximum benefit, and may have other serious repercussions. All horses should be wormed regularly in accordance with the drug manufacturer's instructions. Refer to Chapter 2 for more detail on this issue.

Teeth. These must be rasped at least once a year. The molars develop sharp edges as a result of wear. These sharp edges can affect a horse's ability to chew his food and may also lead to bit evasions.

BRINGING THE HORSE UP FROM GRASS

Most competition and riding horses have a break, spending either some or all of the time at grass. Hunters have their break in the summer months and event horses tend to have their long rest in the winter. The duration of a horse's holiday depends upon the severity and pressure of his competitive career. A horse used for riding activities and gentle hacking will only need a short break from time to time, if he needs a rest at all.

A horse who has hunted three times a fortnight for the whole season will benefit from a complete break of approximately three months at grass in the summer. Assuming that the horse has been out at grass for some time, we'll discuss how to bring him up in preparation for a fitness programme.

Introduce stabling. Bring the horse in for a few hours daily to help him get used to being confined again. Always ensure that there is ample fresh air by keeping the top door of the stable open. Use dust-free bedding and soaked hay to prevent coughing. Gradually increase the time he is stabled until he is only being turned out during the day. All working horses should be turned out daily where possible.

Introduce exercise. Start with 20 minutes at walk to accustom the horse to being handled, gently stimulate heart and breathing rates and tone up the muscles.

Introduce short feed. While the horse is stabled he should have hay to provide roughage and prevent boredom. As work is introduced, he'll need to be fed concentrates. The amount will depend upon the size and type of horse and his condition. Remember to introduce all changes gradually to allow the digestive system a period of adjustment and keep the amount fed in relation to the amount of work being done.

Start grooming. If working a grass-kept horse he can have minimal attention in terms of grooming. His feet must be picked out daily and when he is to be exercised, the saddle and bridle areas must be brushed clean to prevent chafing. However, as he spends more time stabled, the grooming can be increased. He may also need clipping and trimming. If it is cold, he'll need to be rugged up.

This programme of bringing the horse gradually from a grass-kept state to being stabled allows for a period of adjustment. It need not take very long and the amount of time taken will depend very much on individual circumstances. As an approximate guide, 7–10 days should be adequate, but the longer he has been on holiday, the longer the period of adjustment required.

ITQ 131 List six factors that affect the duration of the fittening programme.

THE FITTENING PROCESS

Having undertaken the necessary preparatory work, we now move on to the actual fittening process. Traditionally, there was one main method of fittening a horse. However, with developments in techniques used for fittening human athletes, programmes other than the traditional one have been developed for horses. Interval training is the most important and frequently used of the alternative methods.

Generally speaking, many trainers use a combination of the traditional programme and the interval training programme. We will start by looking at the traditional programme.

A TRADITIONAL PROGRAMME

When planning a fittening programme (of whatever sort) and calculating the time needed to achieve the required level of fitness, it is necessary to know the date of your first main event. For the purposes of this example, we'll assume that this is to be a British Eventing Novice Horse Trial. As an approximate guide, once he has been brought up from grass, 12 weeks should be sufficient time in which to produce a horse ready for this level of competition.

We will work through this programme on a week-by-week basis.

Weeks 1 and 2

The horse will start off in 'soft' condition. His muscles lack tone, his lungs will be incapable of working to full capacity, his heart is not at its most efficient and be may be overweight.

All the early work should be done at walk, usually along the road. If there are suitable tracks to ride around, so much the better, as roads are not the safest of places. Unfortunately however, there is often no alternative.

Walk exercise increases the blood supply throughout the body, thus improving the supply of oxygen to the muscles. As the horse is not being subjected to excessive work he doesn't have to respire anaerobically and is therefore not likely to produce lactic acid (A build-up of which could cause tying up). The gradual increase in circulation ensures that the muscles are conditioned and toned in preparation for the harder work to follow over the next few weeks.

All the systems affected by fittening and training work, i.e. cardiovascular, skeletal and muscular systems, are gradually developed without being overstressed.

This preparation reduces the risk of injury, especially if carried out on a reasonably flat, level surface (rough, uneven or heavy ground should be avoided).

At first 20 minutes a day will be enough, but this should be increased gradually until, by the end of the second week, the horse is being walked for at least one and a half hours a day. As the walking exercise progresses, so body fat is used up and the muscles begin to tone up and develop – note that fat is *not* converted into muscle.

Ensure that the horse walks out actively and straight – he should not be allowed to dawdle. When out hacking, always use knee boots as protection, in case the horse should stumble. Road studs can be fitted to prevent slipping and an exercise sheet provides warmth. Reflective clothing on both horse and rider will improve their visibility, especially in the winter.

Although this introductory process suits most horses there are some who, after a lengthy holiday, feel extremely exuberant, making it unsafe to mount up and attempt to walk around the lanes. In such cases, it is better to lunge on a good surface and let the horse use up some energy without the rider on board. Change the rein regularly to reduce the risk of muscle or tendon strain. Once the horse has settled (and this may take several days) walk work can safely begin. Alternatively, if a horse-walker is available, start the horse off with 5 minutes a day on each rein, building up to a total of 20–30 minutes in a good, strong walk.

Weeks 3 and 4

Begin suppling work at walk in the school and introduce short spells of slow trotting. Approximately 20 minutes schooling before or after an hour of exercise, three times a week, should be sufficient.

The horse may be lunged two or three times a week, avoiding very small circles, which place strain on the limbs. Lunge sessions must be kept short – 10 minutes initially building up to approximately 20 minutes.

Under saddle, introduce steady trotting on good going only and, if possible, slightly uphill. Once the horse is able to trot up a long slope without getting out of breath, he may begin slow canter work.

ITQ 132 Why is the early walk work so important?

Weeks 5 and 6

Short spells of canter are now introduced while schooling or hacking – avoid very hard or deep ground. Keep to good going only, to reduce the risk of concussion or strain. Keep the canter steady and start off cantering for very short periods, (1 or 2 minutes). Check the horse's respiratory rate after each canter – if he is not blowing, the next canter can be a bit stronger and a minute longer.

The horse may be keen to go faster than required but it must be remembered that his limbs, heart and wind are not yet ready; he must therefore be kept to a steady pace.

Don't canter on the lunge at this stage as the horse's muscles and tendons are not yet prepared for the extra strain this would exert.

It may be useful to enter a local dressage competition to help gauge your schooling progress and give you an idea of what to work on at home. Gymnastic jumping may also begin – gridwork is an excellent means of suppling the horse, but it is quite demanding and should not be overdone.

Weeks 7 and 8

Four schooling sessions per week should be sufficient. This work can be kept fresh by interspersing it with lungeing, gridwork and hacking.

Build up the canter work when out hacking – make it stronger than a school working canter and continue to check the horse's breathing after each canter to determine whether he is gaining fitness and ready to do more.

The horse should now be ready to take part in a local showjumping competition.

Weeks 9 and 10

The horse should now be starting to feel fairly fit. As an approximate guide, the canter work should, by now, have been built up to three sessions of 3 minutes strong canter with a break of 3 minutes walk between each. However, aim to canter not more than every fourth day. Excessive canter work is not necessary and leads to wear and tear on the joints and tendons.

Weeks 11 and 12

Taking into account the factors which affect a horse's ability to achieve fitness, by the end of 12 weeks fittening work the horse should be fit enough to compete in a British Eventing Novice Horse Trial. More time would be needed if working towards an Intermediate or Advanced competition, because of the extra length of the courses and increased speeds.

Tables 13 and 14 in this chapter show the daily fitness work – the first 12 weeks would prepare a horse for a Novice event, weeks 13–17 in Table 14 work up to Advanced three-day event level. However, all such information must be used for guidance only – don't be dogmatic when designing a fitness programme.

INTERVAL TRAINING

You will have noticed throughout the traditional fittening programme that references are very approximate when talking about the speed and duration of the canter and the respiratory rates. No exact parameters are given – in order to be successful the trainer would have to be experienced and know when to increase a horse's workload and by how much. There are many top-class trainers who rely purely on their experience, instinctive knowledge and feel for their horses when fittening them for competition. However, for most people, a structured training programme provides an important framework around which to work whilst gaining valuable knowledge and experience, and many prefer the greater certainty of a 'scientific' approach. This is where interval training plays an important role.

Interval training is a technique which, if used with adequate preparation and planning, helps to take some of the guesswork out of getting a horse fit. Originally devised for use by human athletes, interval training consists of set work periods at a specified gait and speed, interspersed with set rest periods. During each walking rest period the horse is allowed to recover partially before being asked to work again.

Advantages of Interval Training

- As the work periods are kept short, the risks of injury and fatigue are reduced.

- The nature of interval training gradually increases the horse's tolerance of work, so reducing stress.

- Interval training is highly effective in developing the horse's aerobic capacity.

- Since the work periods are kept short, the risk of lactic acid build-up as a result of anaerobic respiration is reduced. Furthermore, should any lactic acid be produced, the walk rest period allows its removal from the muscles via the bloodstream.

- Close monitoring of the pulse and respiratory rates gives a positive and definite guide to the level of stress undergone by the horse.

- Riding over the set distance in a set time helps to develop the rider's feel for speed and pacing.

Preparation for Interval Training

1. The horse needs to complete approximately 4 weeks of basic fitness work before commencing an interval training programme.

2. Take and record the horse's temperature, pulse and rate of respiration before exercise, while he is standing under tack. It is a good idea to do this for a few consecutive days to gauge what is normal for each individual horse.

3. Find a suitable area, such as an all-weather gallop, long, wide verge or edge of a large field and measure a distance or distances of 400 m (440 yards). This measurement is to enable correct speeds to be calculated. Therefore, mark the start and finish of each 400 m section clearly.

4. Each 400 m section is to be covered in a set time, according to the speed required.

5. You will need a stopwatch to time yourself over the distance and for timing the pulse and respiratory rates.

6. Keep a record of your programme and the readings.

Time over 400 m	Speed mpm (metres per minute)
1 min 49 sec	220 mpm – brisk trot
1 min 9 sec	350 mpm – steady canter
1 min	400 mpm – slightly stronger canter
57 sec	425 mpm – strong canter

Table 12 Training speeds

ITQ 133 Define 'interval training'.

Starting the Programme

Start off with trot work in or around the fifth week of the fitness programme. Warm up at walk for at least 15 minutes. The following is an example of an initial session:

1	Trot for 2 minutes at 220 mpm
2	Walk for 3 minutes
3	Trot for 2 minutes
4	Halt and record pulse and respiratory rates
5	Walk for 10 minutes
6	Halt and record pulse and respiratory rates

IT session 1

If keeping a written record, this could be presented as:

IT SESSION 1

Date:

1	2	3	4	5	6
(2)	3	(2)	Pulse: Resp:	10	Pulse: Resp:

Note: In Table 13 (later this chapter) the above work session is shown as 'trot 2 x 2 min' (see Monday of week 5).

ITQ 134 What is the purpose of measuring and marking out a 400 m distance?

Terminology

In order to make sense of the sample work sessions, explanation of the terminology is necessary.

Work intervals. Periods 1 and 3 on the example (IT Session 1, above) may be expressed as the work intervals. The number of work intervals per session is known as **repetitions**.

Relief intervals. The 3-minute walk (period 2 in the example) is the relief interval. Once the horse has achieved a certain level of fitness the rider may choose to trot gently between canter work intervals. This is known as **work relief**. It has been proved in fitness trials that, during steady trotting, the pulse and respiratory rates will lower very effectively and lactic acid will be removed from the system efficiently.

Pulse and respiratory rates. The rates are first taken and recorded as soon as the horse finishes the work interval (shown at period 4). The rates are taken again after the recovery period (period 6).

Recovery period. This is the 10-minute walk (period 5) as specified.

Recovery rate. The recovery rate is the rate at which the circulatory and respiratory systems decrease from the working levels (recorded at period 4 in the sample session) to the base rate levels. The reading at period 6 indicates how well the horse has recovered.

Tacking the horse up and bringing him out of the stable causes an increase in pulse and respiration in comparison to the resting rates. Walking to the exercise area (assuming it is fairly close to the yard) will increase the heart rate to between 60–80 bpm (beats per minute). This increased rate must be noted and used as a **base rate** – every horse is different and the normal for each horse should be noted.

Count the breaths per minute once at the exercise area – walking to the exercise area should not cause a noticeable increase in respiratory rate.

When a horse is fit and finding each workout easy, he'll recover within the 10- minute period almost back to his base rates. (He will not return completely to his 'at rest' rates because of the general stimulation of being out of the stable.)

By way of example, if back to base rate, he has recovered fully. If rates are midway between those of period 4 and the base rate, he is only half recovered. These measurements can be used as a basis for estimating the level of fitness achieved.

In the fit horse, his heart rate should fall to below 68 bpm within 10 minutes of completing strenuous exercise.

Training distance. A 400 m unit is the training distance. If using an all-weather gallop, it may be easier to use furlongs as a measurement. One furlong = one-eighth of a mile (approx. 200 m).

Training time. This is the time taken to cover the training distance. In our example, IT session 1, the training time is 1 min 49 sec, resulting in a **training speed** of 220 mpm.

Developing the Programme
Gradually, the trot work can be built up and may be recorded thus:

IT SESSION 8

Date:

(3) 3 (3) 3 (3) 3 (3)   Pulse: 10   Pulse:

                    Resp: Resp:

Or it may be recorded as: trot 4 x 3 min.

                        P1:   R1:

                        P2:   R2:

Every horse will achieve fitness at a different rate. When the horse is coping well with the workout, i.e. recovering quickly, the trot work can be increased. This is done by increasing the time for which the horse trots, but reducing the number of repetitions, as shown below:

IT SESSION 9

Date:

(5) 3 (5) 3 (5)   Pulse: 10   Pulse:

             Resp: Resp:

(Trot 3 x 5 min)

When the horse is coping well with session 9, the canter work can be introduced. This may be recorded thus:

IT SESSION 10

Date:

Warm up for 30 minutes at walk and trot.

(canter at 350 mpm.....minutes)

(1min 9) 3 (1min 9)   Pulse: 10   Pulse:

                   Resp: Resp:

(Canter 2 x 1 min 9 @ 350 mpm)

Once the horse is coping well with this session, the canter can be built up:

IT SESSION 11

Date:

(3) 3 (3)   Pulse: 10   Pulse:

         Resp: Resp:

(Canter 2 x 3 min @ 350 mpm)

Once he is recovering quickly from this session, the canter can be made slightly stronger:

IT SESSION 12

Date:
(Canter at 400 mpm)

(3) 3 (3) 3 (3)	Pulse:	10	Pulse:
	Resp:		Resp:

(Canter 3 x 3 min @ 400 mpm)

In British Eventing Novice horse trials the speed required on the cross-country phase is 520 mpm. In the last IT session before the first event, replace the third 3-minute canter with 2 minutes at 500 mpm.

The Importance of Pulse Rate

The pulse rate indicates the level of stress. If, after work, the horse has a pulse rate of:

100 beats per minute – he has not worked hard enough.

120 beats per minute – a good level of work has been attained.

150 beats per minute – too much stress has been exerted.

200 beats per minute – the horse will be respiring anaerobically.

WEEK	MONDAY	TUESDAY	WEDNESDAY	THURSDAY	FRIDAY	SATURDAY	SUNDAY
1 and 2	\u2014\u2014\u2014\u2014\u2014\u2014\u2014\u2014\u2014\u2014\u2014 Build up from 20 minutes walking daily to 1½ hr \u2014\u2014\u2014\u2014\u2014\u2014\u2014						
3	Hack (walk) 1 hr	School 20 min Hack 1 hr	Hack 1 hr	School 20 min Hack 1 hr	Hack 1½ hr	School 20 min Hack 1 hr	Rest
4	Hack 1¼ hr Introduce slow trot	Lunge 10 min Hack 45 min	School 20 min Hack 1 hr	Lunge 10 min School 20 min Hack 30 min	Hack 1½ hr Increase trot work	School 20 min Hack 1 hr	Rest
5	Hack 1½ hr Trot 2 x 2 min 3 min walk in between	Lunge 10 min School 20 min Hack 30 min	School 30 min Hack I hr	As Tuesday	School 30 min Hack 1 hr Trot 3 x 2 min	Hack 1½ hr	Rest
6	Lunge 15 min Hack 1¼ hr	School 45 min inc. gridwork Hack 30 min	Hack 1½ hr Trot 3 x 3 min	Lunge 15 min School 30 min Hack 30 min	As Monday Canter 2 x 1 min 9 @ 350 mpm	As Tuesday	Rest
7	School 40 min Hack 1 hr	Hack 1½ hr Trot 3 x 3 min Canter 2 x 3 min	School 45 min inc. gridwork Hack 30 min	Lunge 15 min School 30 min Hack 30 min	School 30 min Hack 1 hr Trot 3 x 3 min	Dressage competition	Rest

8	School 30 min Hack 1¹/₄ hr	Hack inc. canter 2 x 3 min	Lunge 15 min School 30 min	School 45 min inc. gridwork	Show-jumping competition	Rest	Hack 1¹/₂ hr Canter 2 x 4 min
9 and 10	School 30 min Hack 1¹/₄ hr	Cross-country schooling Hack 30 min	School 30 min Hack 1 hr	Hack inc. canter 3 x 3 min	Hack 1¹/₂ hr	Show-jumping competition	Rest
11 and 12	School 30 min Hack 1 hr inc. trot 3 x 3 min	Hack 1¹/₂ hr inc. canter 2 x 3 min @ 400 mpm,1 x 2 min @ 500 mpm	Hack 1¹/₂ hr Walk	School 30 min Hack 1 hr	School 45 min inc. gridwork Hack 45 min	One-day Event	Rest

Table 13 Interval training programme to Novice level

Table 13 gives an indication of suggested work. Obviously this may not suit every horse and rider – it is not always possible to keep to a definite routine. The programme can be adapted to suit individual circumstances.

ITQ 135 What is meant by a 'relief interval'?

Points to Remember

- Without knowing the pulse rates, progress cannot be monitored accurately. The rider can, however, judge the respiratory rate without dismounting.

- The ground conditions will affect the programme; very deep going makes movement much harder work and increases the risk of injury.

- Undulating, hilly ground also increases the stress factor.

- With regard to the above, be flexible and alter the programme as necessary to suit individual horses, ground conditions, etc.

- Keep a written record of your programme for future reference.

- Training sessions should be carried out at four-day intervals – never more frequently as this would over-stress the horse and not allow him to recover from one workout before the next.

- The sessions may be incorporated into the 'traditional' fittening programme.

- Do not increase the workload until the horse is recovering well within the 10- minute relief period.

WEEK	MONDAY	TUESDAY	WEDNESDAY	THURSDAY	FRIDAY	SATURDAY	SUNDAY
1 and 2	——————————————Build up from 30 minutes walking daily to 1½ hr——————————————						
3	Hack (walk) 1½ hr	School 20 min Hack 1 hr	Hack 1½ hr	School 20 min Hack 1 hr	Hack 1½ hr	School 20 min Hack 1 hr	Rest
4	Hack 1¼ hr Introduce slow trot	Lunge 10 min Hack 45 min	School 20 min Hack 1 hr	Lunge 10 min School 20 min Hack 30 min	Hack 1½ hr Increase trot work	School 20 min Hack 1 hr	Rest
5	Hack 1½ hr Trot 2 x 2 min 3 min walk in between	Lunge 10 min School 20 min Hack 30 min	School 30 min Hack 1 hr	As Tuesday	School 30 min Hack 1 hr Trot 3 x 2 min	Hack 1½ hr	Rest
6	Lunge 15 min Hack 1¼ hr	School 45 min inc. gridwork Hack 30 min	Hack 1½ hr Trot 3 x 3 min	Lunge 15 min School 30 min Hack 30 min	As Monday Introduce short canter on hack	As Tuesday	Rest
7	School 40 min Hack 1 hr	Hack 1½ hr Trot 3 x 3 min Canter 2 x 3 min	School 45 min inc. gridwork Hack 30 min	Lunge 15 min School 30 min Hack 30 min	School 30 min Hack 1 hr Trot 3 x 3 min	Dressage competition	Rest
8	School 30 min Hack 1¼ hr	Hack inc. canter 2 x 3 min	Lunge 15 min School 30 min	School 45 min inc. gridwork	Showjumping competition	Rest	Hack 1½ hr Canter 2 x 4 min
9	School 30 min Hack 1¼ hr	Cross-country schooling Hack 30 min	School 30 min Hack 1 hr	Hack inc canter 3 x 4 min	Hack 1½ hr	Showjumping competition	Rest
10	School 30 min Hack 1 hr inc. trot 3 x 3 min	Hack 1½ hr inc. canter 3 x 4 @ 400 mpm	Hack 1½ hr Walk	School 30 min Hack 1 hr	School 45 min inc. gridwork Hack 45 min	One-day Event	Rest
11	Hack 1½ hr Walk	School 30 min Hack 45 min	Hack inc. canter 3 x 6 min	Hack 2 hr Walk	School 45 min inc. gridwork Hack 30 min	School 40 min hack 1 hr	One-day event
12	Rest	Hack 2 hr	School 40 min Hack 1 hr	Canter (400 mpm) 2 x 6 min 1 x 7 min	School 30 min Hack 1½ hr	School 40 min Hack 1¼ hr	As Friday
13	Rest	Hack 2hr	Canter (400mph) 3 x 7 min (last 3 min @ 500 mpm)	School 20 min Hack 1½ hr	School 30 min Hack 1½ hr	School 45 min inc. gridwork Hack 1½ hr	One-day event

14	Rest	Hack 2 hr	School 30 min Hack 1 hr	School 20 min canter 4 x 7 min	Hack 2 hr	School 1 hr Hack 1 hr	Rest
15	School 45 min Hack 45 min	Canter 3 x 8 min (last 4 min @ 500 mpm)	School 20 min Hack 1 hr	School 45 min inc. gridwork Hack 1 hr	School 45 min	School 1 hr Hack 30 min Travel to event	One-day event
16	Rest	School 30 min Hack 1 hr	School 45 min Hack 45 min	Canter 1 x 8 min@ 400 mpm 1 x 8 min @ 500 mpm 1 x 8 min @ 650 mpm	School 20 min Hack 1 hr	School 40 min Hack 45 min	Rest
17	School 45 min inc. gridwork	Travel to event Hack 1 hr	School 1 hr Hack 1 hr	Dressage work Quiet hack 1 hr	Dressage	Speed and endurance	Show-jumping

Table 14 Interval training programme to Advanced level

ITQ 136 In terms of pulse and respiratory rates, what is meant by the 'base rate'?

ITQ 137 During an interval training session, when are the pulse and respiratory rates taken?

ITQ 138 What is the main indication that a horse has recovered well after an interval training session?

ITQ 139 How often should interval training be carried out?

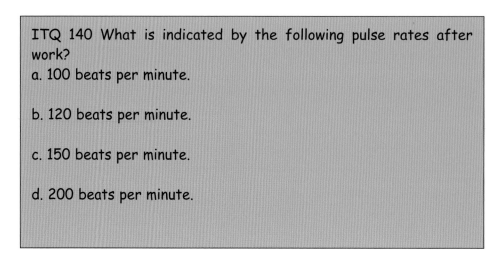

ITQ 140 What is indicated by the following pulse rates after work?

a. 100 beats per minute.

b. 120 beats per minute.

c. 150 beats per minute.

d. 200 beats per minute.

Interval Training to Advanced Levels

So far, we have discussed the fittening programme to prepare a horse for a BE Novice horse trial. At Advanced levels the horse has to be much fitter, especially if working towards a three-day event. Table 14 shows one example of an interval training programme to Advanced level.

After 6 weeks of toning up and basic fittening the canter workouts can be built up (see Table 15). Some trainers advocate building up the work intervals to three sessions of ten minutes at 400 mpm and only introducing fast work in the last three weeks. It may prove too much for some horses to canter for three sessions of 10 minutes at a stretch. In such cases, the training time is reduced and the speed slightly increased.

WEEK	DAY	CANTER WORKOUTS
7	(Tues)	2 x 3 min @ 400 mpm
8	(Tues)	2 x 3 min @ 400 mpm
	(Sun)	2 x 4 min @ 400 mpm
9	(Thurs)	3 x 4 min @ 400 mpm
10	(Tues)	3 x 5 min @ 400 mpm
		1 x 5 min @ 500 mpm
11	(Weds)	3 x 6 min @ 450 mpm
12	(Thurs)	2 x 6 min @ 400 mpm
		1 x 7 min: 3 min @ 400 mpm
		4 min @ 500 mpm
13	(Wed)	3 x 7 min: 4 min @ 400 mpm
		3 min @ 500 mpm
14	(Thurs)	4 x 7 min: 3 min @ 400 mpm
		4 min @ 500 mpm
15	(Tues)	3 x 8 min: 3 min @ 400 mpm
		5 min @ 500 mpm

Note: Some horses may be suited to shorter bursts of work, e.g. 6 or 7 x 5 min instead.		
16	(Thurs)	1 x 8 min @ 400 mpm 1 x 8 min @ 500 mpm 1 x 8 min @ 650 mpm
As mentioned above, 7 x 5 min may suit certain horses better than 3 x 8 min.		
17		Three Day Event

Table 15 A summary of the latter stages of an interval training programme to Advanced three-day event level

OTHER METHODS OF CONDITIONING

In addition to interval training, there are other methods of training (conditioning) the horse. These include:

- Endurance training
- Sprint training
- The speed test system.

ENDURANCE TRAINING

Endurance training takes the form of slow-speed, long-distance exercise. The heart rate is maintained under 150 bpm, all tissue respiration is aerobic and there is no lactic acid accumulation.

Endurance training is used for fittening the horse for long-distance competitions or for the initial weeks of an interval or traditional fitness programme.

Endurance training:

- improves the aerobic capacity of the horse
- delays the onset of fatigue
- increases skeletal and tendon strength.

Sample Programme

This is a sample 10-week programme, working the horse for five or six days per week.

Week 1	Initial walk period: 20–30 minutes daily.
Week 2	Build up to 60 minutes roadwork. Include gentle trotting and short burst of trot.
Week 3	60–90 minutes walk and trot, gradually increasing the length of time trotting.
Week 4	90 minutes walk and trot. Short canter on flat ground.
Weeks 5–6	Increase the distance: build up to approximately 13–16 km (8–10 miles) per day for approximately four days per week.
Week 7	Continue above work. Include work on hilly terrain if possible.
Weeks 8–10	Continue distance work: average approximately 13 km (10 miles) per hour. Start to include canter: aim to increase the heart rate to 120–150 bpm for approximately 45–60 minutes.

TRADITIONAL RACING TRAINING

This is the traditional method of fittening horses for point-to-pointing and jump training. It involves much slow canter work over long distances, with fast work performed once or twice a week.

This method:

- Builds up the horse's aerobic capacity during the periods of slow work.
- Develops the anaerobic capacity through the fast work. (i.e. it makes the body more able to cope with the effects of lactate accumulation).

This method of conditioning can be quite stressful to the systems of the horse as a considerable amount of work is done. While it has produced some excellent results over the years, it is noticeable that many trainers nowadays are modifying traditional methods with the introduction of practices associated with interval training.

Sample Programme

Weeks 1–4 The initial endurance training. Roadwork, building up to 90 minutes of walk and trot, gradually increasing the trotting periods.

Weeks 5–6 Approximately 1.6 km (1 mile) steady canter twice per week.

Week 7 Approximately 3.2 km (2miles) steady canter twice per week.

Weeks 8–10 Approximately 4.8 km (3 miles) steady canter (increase speed last half mile) twice per week. 1 uphill sprint per week (if possible).

Note: The horse works six days per week. On non-canter days he would be hacked.

THE SPEED TEST SYSTEM

This fittening programme has been adapted from a system used successfully by human athletes and may be tailored to meet the differing needs of the various types of competition horse.

Basically, the speed test system is a three-stage programme:

1. First stage consists of a long foundation stage (approximately 12 weeks). At the end of this stage a speed test is carried out.
2. Second stage – gallop work is introduced and, after approximately 6 weeks, a second speed test is carried out.
3. Third stage – competition conditions are simulated.

The length of the overall programme is dependent upon the horse's ability to achieve fitness (the influence of breeding, age, previous fitness, etc.)

First stage. As with other fittening programmes, the first stage consists of a foundation of slow work. The first 2 weeks are spent at walk, after which slow trotting is introduced. The trot work is built up to approximately 3.2 km (2 miles) per day. This is built up further and canter work is introduced.

Within this foundation stage, which may last approximately 12 weeks, the canter is built up so that on every third day the horse is cantered for approximately 10 km (6½ miles). The work on the other two days should be easier and for a shorter duration.

The workload is determined on a four-week cycle:
- one week of moderate work
- one week of hard work
- one moderate week
- followed by an easy week.

A heart rate monitor is used to ensure that the horse never becomes distressed. The duration of the canter periods will be determined by the horse's heart rate and the onset of fatigue – if the horse feels tired he must be allowed to rest and recover.

Second stage. This starts at the end of the three-month period, when short gallops are introduced. This is where the programme gains its other title, 'The Fartlek System' – *fartlek* is the Swedish word used to describe the short gallops. These gallops are run over varying short distances. The horse is never galloped in 'easy' weeks and never more than twice a week.

Before moving on to the second stage, a speed test is used to assess the horse's level of fitness. The horse is galloped at a moderate speed over a distance of approximately 4 km (2^1/$_2$ miles). At this stage the heart rate monitor is invaluable for judging the degree of stress – if the heart rate goes too high the rider can slow down. An eventer is galloped for approximately one minute to push the heart rate up to 190–200 bpm. The heart rate is recorded and compared to previous readings. If the heart rate is low (around 160 bpm, followed by rapid recovery) the horse is fit enough to move on to the second stage.

The second stage lasts for approximately 6 weeks and is designed to develop further the respiratory and muscular structures. This involves increasing the fast work; an eventer may do a 3–4.8 km (2–3 mile) gallop, the speed of which is adapted to keep the heart rate below 180 beats per minute. This fast work is carried out twice a week, but never during a moderate or easy week.

After approximately six weeks another speed test is carried out over an increased distance.

Third stage. At this stage the competition conditions are simulated – the duration is decreased and the speed increased. A racehorse would be worked in intervals with gallops of about half a mile (just under 1 km) at racing pace, interspersed with trot work until the heart and respiratory rates have lowered. He would undergo such a test four days before a race.

An eventer is worked at speed over distances which in total are close to those of the level of the competition. For example, an Advanced horse would do three 1 km (five-furlong) gallops at steeplechase speed, while a novice horse would work at Novice eventing speed over shorter distances.

The speed test method of fittening is fairly flexible and provides variation throughout the programme, which helps to relieve boredom. It is, however, important that records are kept to gauge the horse's progress and that a great deal of common sense is used in determining whether the horse is becoming fatigued or not. If used properly by a knowledgeable trainer, this system can achieve great fittening effects whilst avoiding the undesirable effects of fatigue.

VARIABLE FACTORS IN TRAINING PROGRAMMES

As previously mentioned, it is impossible to write down an exact programme that would suit every horse, as each is unique in his ability to achieve fitness. Also, riders and trainers have access to varying standards and types of facilities. For example, some riders don't have a hill in their county so to say 'you *must* include short bursts uphill' is futile.

Any interval training programme must be flexible enough to allow for adaptations when a continuing four-day cycle cannot be adhered to. For example the training time, speed and number of repetitions may have to be reduced to prevent over-stressing the limbs, heart, etc. on the occasions when there are not three clear days between workouts and competitions. This will inevitably occur when the horse is competing regularly on a weekly basis.

In most programmes the fast work is only introduced in the last 3 weeks or so and should never be carried out 'flat out'. A three-quarter speed gallop over a distance of approximately 500 m (two and a half furlongs) will develop strength and speed while a longer, slower gallop of say half-speed over 800 m (four furlongs) will develop endurance.

The speed test system is very demanding as the horses work at close to competition speeds in the third stage.

Whatever system is chosen it is essential to treat every horse as an individual and find out which programme best suits each.

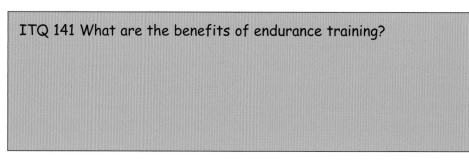

ITQ 141 What are the benefits of endurance training?

ITQ 142 What are the benefits of traditional race training?

OTHER AIDS TO FITTENING

There are several other training aids can be used as appropriate to supplement the ridden exercise.

Horse-walkers are useful for warming up and cooling down a number of horses using minimal manpower. They are becoming increasingly popular on busy yards. The main disadvantage of the horse-walker is the element of boredom. It is also important that the direction is changed regularly to prevent horses becoming one-sided.

Treadmills are not so popular as horse-walkers, but are useful for working one horse. The horse wears a harness and the treadmill is set at a specific speed. The harness prevents the horse from falling in the event of a power failure, which may cause the treadmill to stop suddenly.

The treadmill speed can be increased gradually over a period of time to prepare the horse and then, under experienced supervision, used safely at speeds of up to approximately 40 kph (25 mph). Treadmills can also be inclined up to 10 degrees, making the work more demanding.

Swimming offers an alternative/complementary method of training the equine athlete. It provides a strenuous activity ideal for developing cardiopulmonary capacity and it is a useful way of exercising young racehorses or injured horses without stressing the limbs. As the horse's limbs are not bearing weight there is no jarring effect. This does mean however that the limbs do not become strengthened through swimming – for limbs to strengthen there must be some weight-bearing activity.

The initial swimming sessions must be kept short to avoid anxiety and tension. All pools should have a safe ramp in and out. Some pools consist of a straight swimway only, while others are circular. The horse is guided through the pool by assistants holding lines attached to the cavesson.

If properly integrated into a training regime, swimming can be a valuable addition to the fitness programme. To further increase the heart rate the horse can be made to swim against a current.

ITQ 143 State two benefits of swimming as a method of exercise.

CHAPTER SUMMARY

It may be that you will have fittened many horses for different disciplines and you may use very similar programmes to those described here. Conversely, your fittening programme may be nothing like those described here but, if the horse achieves full fitness, then the programme works – that's the important thing. The main point to consider is that every horse is an individual and as trainers, we all have slightly different methods of fittening horses.

If you have not fittened many horses to date, then this chapter will have introduced you to some important principles. Having studied it you should, hopefully, feel able to plan and implement fitness programmes for different levels and types of competition.

CHAPTER 9

MANAGEMENT OF THE FITNESS PROGRAMME

The aims and objectives of this chapter are to explain:

- The day-to-day management associated with the fittening routine, including feeding, exercise, grooming and health care.
- How to monitor the stages of fitness throughout the programme through physical development, soundness and condition.
- How to monitor heart rate as a means of assessing fitness.
- What to check on a day-to-day basis in terms of assessing fitness.
- When and how to modify a fitness programme.

Having designed a suitable fitness programme it has to be implemented on a day-to-day basis.

THE DAILY FITTENING ROUTINE

FEEDING

Nutrition is one of the most important aspects of any fitness routine. It has already been discussed in Chapters 3–6, so a brief summary of the main points will suffice here.

- Estimate the horse's bodyweight and calculate his maximum daily food intake and necessary energy and protein requirements.

- The ratio of forage to concentrates will depend on the horse's level of work – initially he will probably require 60 per cent forage and 40 per cent concentrates as his workload will be of a medium level. As his fitness work progresses and the workload increases, so the ratio will alter – increase the concentrates and slightly decrease the forage.

- Ration calculations are made easier if compound feeds such as event cubes or coarse mixes are used. These contain the correct balance of protein and digestible energy for horses in energetic work.

- The forage ration must be kept as dust-free as possible to ensure that the respiratory system functions efficiently. Some horses are sensitive to the dust mites and spores found in hay – the hay must therefore be soaked for 10 minutes to prevent dust from being inhaled. If soaking the hay doesn't ease the horse's allergy, an alternative forage such as vacuum-packed hay or haylage must be used. In extreme cases it may be necessary to feed the forage ration through the use of hay cubes.

- Give four smaller feeds per day rather than three large ones. This will prevent boredom and, as the horse's stomach is relatively small, will ensure the stomach is not over-stretched.

- Provide a salt and mineral lick in the stable and on days when the horse has sweated, add two tablespoons of salt to a feed. Electrolytes can be fed just before and after a competition to replace the minerals lost through sweating.

- Occasionally, horses receiving large quantities of concentrates will lose their appetite and fail to clear up each feed. Having ruled out any other reason for not eating up, e.g. ill-health, it may be necessary to reduce the amount of concentrates temporarily and increase the forage ration. Reduce the hard concentrates and add tempting and easily digestible feedstuffs such as boiled barley and sliced carrots.

EXERCISE

- The fittening programme will ensure that the horse is exercised daily. Additional exercise in the form of turning out helps to keep the horse mentally relaxed and prevents the legs from filling. Turning the horse out after a strenuous workout or competition is the ideal way to loosen him up and ease stiffness.

- On his rest day the horse should be turned out for as long as possible to prevent boredom. Obviously, fields should be safely fenced with post and rails, and horses turned out in small groups, preferably pairs, who get on well with each other. Any horse known to kick or bully others should however, be turned out alone to prevent injuries.

- As mentioned in Chapter 8, horse-walkers are another means of exercising and, while not the most interesting method for the horse, they provide a labour-saving way of exercising several horses at the same time.

- Daily exercise should be varied to prevent boredom – intersperse schooling with hacking and try to vary the route if possible.

GROOMING

- The horse must have his feet picked out when the stable is mucked out each morning and every time he leaves or enters his stable. Before exercise he must be quartered and, ideally, he should be thoroughly strapped after exercise. Banging or wisping the main muscle masses during strapping helps to tone the muscles and promotes improved circulation and a shiny coat.

- When the weather allows, the horse can be bathed to remove excessive grease and scurf from the coat, mane and tail. After washing, a small amount of baby oil run through the tail will make it easier to brush through without tearing the hairs.

- Between October and March the horse will need to be clipped at least twice to allow him to work without sweating excessively. His mane and tail should be pulled and trimmed.

GENERAL HEALTH

- **Shoeing**. Check the shoes daily when picking out the feet for signs of risen clenches or loosening. The farrier should be booked well in advance.

- **Worming**. This must be carried out regularly and the fields must be kept free of droppings to prevent re-infestation.

- **Condition**. Check that the horse does not lose condition as his workload increases. If he does lose weight, having checked his teeth for sharp edges and ascertained that he is not carrying an undue worm burden, increase the concentrate ration. The horse must not carry too much condition either – this will make it difficult to get him fully fit, especially for fast work, and will put extra strain on his heart, lungs and limbs.

- **Soundness.** The horse's legs must be checked daily for any changes. Know what is normal for each horse so that any new lumps or swellings can be treated. The legs should feel cool and clean – free from any heat or swelling – and the horse should be completely sound. After a strenuous workout or competition, pay extra attention to the legs. If the going has been firm it may be necessary to hose the legs or apply cold packs and support bandages to prevent filling.

- **Temperament**. Fittening and competition work affects horses in different ways. Some are more relaxed when in hard work, while others become 'sharper', possibly even aggressive, when they are fittened. In some cases, this 'aggression' is related not directly to fitness, but to the imposition of a regime that doesn't suit the horse psychologically (e.g. too much time spent stabled) – see Stress, below.

Stress

Stress in some forms is part and parcel of the fitness programme – without stress the body will not adapt and develop. The trainer's skill lies in knowing how much stress, and of what type, to exert – *distress* can lead to damage, both psychological and physical.

Therefore, the horse must be exposed to gradually increasing levels of stress and must be allowed rest periods for recovery to prevent overstressing. Gradual introduction of stress enables the horse's systems to adapt and alter, thereby preparing them for similar levels of stress in the future.

Eventually, the horse will reach his peak of fitness – at this point the stress cannot be increased further without the risk of souring the horse or causing physical damage. Once peak fitness has been achieved, the objective is to maintain it for only as long as is necessary. For example, an eventer doesn't need to be at peak fitness for the whole season – his peak should be reached for the major event or events.

If a horse is overstressed or bored he may develop stereotypical behaviour patterns, so-called 'stable vices', such as weaving, cribbing, biting or kicking. Turning out to grass for a few hours each day helps to reduce boredom and stress.

Through observation, the horse's mental attitude, condition and soundness can be monitored and any adjustments made as necessary. Further to this, I reiterate the point made in Chapter 8, that programmes related to fitness shouldn't be absolutely rigid – while a routine is essential, a little flexibility allows important adjustments to be made.

ITQ 144

a. When checking the horse's legs each day, how should they appear and feel?

b. What signs would indicate a potential problem?

MONITORING TO ASSESS FITNESS

We now move on to look at the ways in which the horse's stage of fitness can be monitored. We need to do this for two fundamental reasons:

1. Simply in order to assess the effectiveness of the fittening programme – this is always essential, but it may become especially significant if the horse is not performing adequately.

2. Because the fitness requirements of each horse will differ along with the level of competition – the trainer has to be able to judge when the optimum fitness level has been reached.

There are several different ways of monitoring fitness, some of which require specialist equipment and expertise.

MONITORING HEART RATE

Monitoring the heart rate is an accurate means of assessing fitness and may be done by the following methods.

Taking the pulse. This is done at a point where an artery passes over bone, close to the surface of the skin. The pulse is normally felt in the sub-mandibular artery on the inner edge of the lower jawbone. It can be difficult to take the rate of a horse who has just exercised strenuously as he may not stand still.

Stethoscope. This is placed just behind the horse's left elbow. In practice it can be difficult to count the heart rate when the horse has worked hard and, as the heart rate drops significantly as soon as work stops, this is not the most accurate way of monitoring heart rate.

Heart rate monitor. The heart rate monitor consists of a small transmitter, with electrodes attaching to the horse's skin at the withers and girth. The electrodes are secured beneath the saddle (or roller, if lungeing) and girth. The monitor, in the form of a wrist watch, can be read instantly by the rider during exercise. This enables an examination of the heart rate at exercise and can be very useful when gauging the process of fitness throughout the fittening programme.

The electrodes detect the electrical impulses which initiate the heart beat. This means that the monitor displays the actual heart rate rather than the pulse. This makes it more effective than taking the pulse as, since the heart rate falls rapidly in the first minute post-exercise, the reading taken on cessation of exercise does not equate to the heart rate during work.

The benefits of using a heart rate monitor can be summarized thus:

1. A heart rate monitor allows the horse to be worked at a specific heart rate.
2. The level of stress exerted on the cardiovascular system can be monitored.
3. The rider can identify the onset of fatigue and reduce the risk of injury. The heart rate increases rapidly as glycogen is depleted – a sign of fatigue.
4. The heart rate monitor is particularly useful during interval training as it gives an accurate readout of the heart rate achieved during exercise and the time taken for the heart rate to recover.

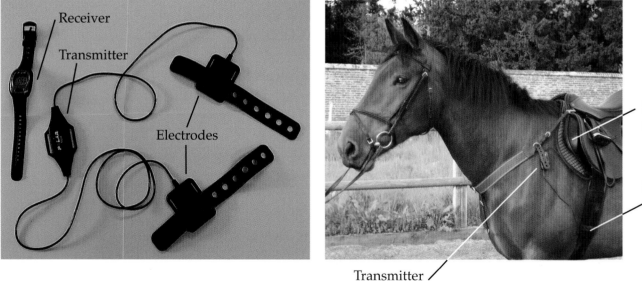

Figure 25 Using a heart rate monitor

Electrocardiogram (ECG). This specialized equipment, used by the vet, can measure and record the level of electrical activity created by the nervous impulses in the heart. The size of the heart can also be gauged as, the larger the heart, the longer it will take to contract. A fit horse will have a slower resting heart rate and less increase in heart rate for any given amount of exercise, and also a quicker recovery rate.

MONITORING WEIGHT

Competition horses cannot perform properly if overweight. While observation is the method frequently used to assess weight gain or loss, it is better to be more precise by using a weighbridge or tape.

Racehorses each have their optimum racing weight – some trainers weigh the horses before and after a race and are able to judge the degree of stress and fluid loss incurred by the horse according to the amount of weight he has lost. Once the optimum racing weight has been determined, efforts are made to maintain it. This practice should be put into context by saying first, that trainers monitor many other physiological indicators in parallel with weighing and second, that consideration is given to the fact that *immature* horses are likely to increase in weight as they mature, strengthen and develop their musculature. However, keeping a record of the weight of any performance horse provides useful data for monitoring fitness.

ITQ 145 Give three reasons why fitness levels need to be monitored.

ITQ 146 List the main benefits of using the heart rate monitor.

DETERMINING THE ANAEROBIC THRESHOLD

As we saw in Chapter 7, lactic acid is produced by fast-twitch low-oxidative (glycolytic) muscle fibres. While the horse respires aerobically, there will be little lactic acid production. However, the point at which the horse begins to respire anaerobically is identified by an increase in the quantity of lactic acid in the bloodstream. This increase (acidosis) will occur when the bloodstream cannot remove it as quickly as it is being produced. This point is known as the **anaerobic threshold**.

The anaerobic threshold will be determined by the horse's level of fitness; the fitter he is, the higher the threshold. A major objective of fittening a horse is to increase the aerobic capacity, thus delaying the point at which lactic acid is produced.

With the use of specialist equipment, it is possible to test the levels of lactic acid in the bloodstream. This is done before exercise starts to establish the normal 'at rest' levels. The horse is then worked at a specific speed for a set time, after which a blood sample is taken and lactate levels determined. This process continues until the anaerobic threshold is met.

The horse is tested throughout his training – once the threshold ceases to rise the horse is at the limit of his lactic acid tolerance, and has therefore reached his peak fitness.

If the threshold starts to fall it may be indicative of over-training or a relapse in fitness, possibly as a result of injury or illness.

Most trainers do not have the specialized equipment needed to measure the anaerobic threshold but, as a general guide, a horse showing a marked increase in respiratory rate after exercise will have respired anaerobically.

BLOOD AND SERUM ANALYSIS

Cells are present in the blood in characteristic proportions and analysis of these proportions helps to assess the state of a horse's health.

To be of real benefit, tests must be taken regularly so that the normal proportions for the individual horse are known. The correct functioning of the organs and level of fitness of the horse may be tested through the analysis of a blood and serum sample in the laboratory. The results are interpreted by the veterinary surgeon and, if necessary, the diet and training programme can be adjusted.

In order to obtain true readings, blood samples must be taken when the horse is at rest before exercise. This is because the spleen acts as a reservoir of blood, releasing this surplus into the system whenever it is under stress, for example, during exercise, which would lead to inaccurate PCV readings (see below).

The absolute number of red and white cells present in the sample can be determined either by microscopic examination of a smear or by sophisticated electronic means. The proportion of blood cells to plasma may be measured as a percentage – this measurement is known as the **packed cell volume (PCV)**. The normal range of PCV is between 34 and 44 per cent. The PCV gives a good indication of fitness and stress levels: if there is a very high percentage PCV, it indicates that the horse is highly excited or suffering from dehydration and/or shock.

Other factors measured are:

RBC. Red blood cell count – the actual number of red blood cells per ml of blood.

Hb. The concentration of haemoglobin g/per ml blood. The haemoglobin in the red blood cells affects their oxygen-carrying capacity.

McV. The mean (average) red cell volume.

McHc. The mean (average) red cell haemoglobin concentration.

McH. The mean (average) red cell haemoglobin content.

WBC. White blood cell count. This is measured with an electronic cell counter. The different types of white blood cells are counted and the analysis is known as the **differential WBC**. The white cells (leucocytes) are concerned with the body's defence mechanism; a normal count indicates that the system is not under challenge.

PV. Plasma viscosity. The thickness of the blood is recorded thus. In conjunction with this, the **erythrocyte sedimentation rate (ESR)** is also recorded. In addition to indicating general unfitness, these two tests can lead to the detection of inflammatory conditions.

Serum Biochemical Tests

There are several serum tests used in fitness testing; as with haematology the biochemical tests are chosen selectively in accordance with specific requirements. The main tests are of the following substances.

Serum proteins. These are albumins and globulins, the levels of which reflect nutritional balance and the efficiency of the digestive tract. Globulin levels tend to rise in response to disease.

Plasma electrolytes. These are the soluble mineral ions present in the plasma. Metabolism is dependent upon a balance of the various minerals.

Enzymes. Metabolism is also affected by enzymes – biochemical catalysts. Normal enzyme levels indicate efficient metabolism. The enzymes most often tested for are **CK, SGOT (AST)** and **Gamma GT**.

– CK (creatine kinase) is an enzyme of the muscles and heart. Levels increase when exertional rhabdomyolysis and some cardiovascular conditions occur.

– SGOT (serum glutamic oxaloacetic transaminase), now termed aminotransferase (AST), is found in all tissues. Its level in serum increases in response to exertional rhabdomyolysis and some liver disorders.

– Gamma GT (gamma glutamyltransferase) is a liver enzyme which may increase gradually as training is built up. If the horse is overstressed the levels increase dramatically.

Blood testing and serum analysis are expensive methods of gauging fitness so it is important that the trainer understands the vet's interpretation of the results and acts accordingly.

ITQ 147 If using blood and serum analysis as a means of assessing a horse's fitness, why is it beneficial to test samples regularly?

ITQ 148 What is meant by PCV?

ITQ 149 What is the normal range of PCV in a healthy horse?

DAY-TO-DAY MONITORING OF FITNESS

The sophisticated methods of fitness assessment described certainly have their place, particularly when monitoring horses at the higher levels of national and international competition. However, on a day-to-day basis, much can be learnt about every horse's fitness status by common sense observation.

In Chapter 7 we looked at the various factors to be considered when appraising a horse's level of fitness. It is these same factors that need to be assessed on a daily basis throughout the fittening programme. In summary, these are:

Physical condition. Loss of condition may be caused through dietary imbalance, sharp teeth preventing efficient mastication, internal parasites, stress or illness. These causes must be eliminated before increasing the feed ration.

Excessive weight gain needs to be rectified through adjustment of the feed ration. The horse should have a healthy appetite, clearing up all of his feeds willingly. He should be bright and alert, showing all of the signs of good health.

Muscle tone and development. The muscles should become more toned and well developed as the horse becomes fitter and stronger.

Respiratory system. The horse should not cough or have whitish/yellow nasal discharge which indicates either an infection or dust allergy. Check other signs of health, e.g. TPR, to determine the cause.

Soundness. The lower legs should feel cold with clean, well-defined tendons and no puffiness. The horse should be 100 per cent sound. Any previous tendon injuries or soundness problems must be taken into account when planning a fittening programme – it will take longer to achieve fitness safely if the horse has had problems in the past.

Temperament. The horse should not shows signs of boredom or stress, e.g. box-walking, weaving, etc. and he should show enthusiasm for his work. Any deviation should be noted. If, for example, a normally keen jumper starts to refuse, it may indicate pain, possibly the start of a bony disorder of the lower leg, or that the horse has become 'stale' and lost his desire to jump for fun. Alternatively, he may have lost confidence. These factors all need to be considered.

A horse who starts to nap and rear midway through training could be in pain through back injury, or similar.

Behaviour/energy levels. These two points have purposefully been put together – so often a horse who has too much energy, i.e. one who is receiving too much high-energy feed for his workload, will be 'badly behaved'. In this case, the energy feeds should be reduced slightly to find the correct balance and the horse's regime examined to see if improvements can be made. Increasing the workload will only be necessary if the fitness programme warrants – If you increase the workload purely to 'use up' his energy, he may get too fit for your requirements. You must use your judgement in such cases.

Alternatively, if the horse seems lacking in energy, the energy-giving feeds will need to be increased gradually. This should only be done after investigation has ruled out other reasons for depression in the horse, e.g. poor health, or pain.

Remember, all changes to the diet should be introduced gradually to allow the digestive tract time to adapt to the altered composition of the feedstuffs. Sudden changes can lead to colic and, if the carbohydrate intake is increased, azoturia and laminitis.

Remember, also, that reducing the workload will have an adverse effect on your fittening programme – it will slow the fittening process, so should be avoided unless the horse is overstressed or 'sour'. This point, however, brings us on to consider those modifications to the fittening programme that may, at times, be necessary.

MODIFIYING THE PROGRAMME

Through your observations and assessments, you will know whether or not the fittening programme is effective and suitable for each individual horse. Depending upon the horse's health and fitness status, there may be occasions when it is necessary to modify the programme in one or more ways.

- If the horse is not progressing at a suitable rate it may be necessary to postpone the first competition and extend the programme. This will also apply if the horse suffers an injury/soundness problem.

- If the horse is not achieving fitness at the desired rate, and there seem to be no adverse underlying reasons, increase the length of the daily workload. If you are using interval training it may be necessary to increase the number of repetitions of work intervals.

- If the horse's respiratory rates are not increasing sufficiently after work intervals, increase the training speeds. Build up the speeds gradually to avoid overstressing the horse.

- If the horse is gaining fitness too quickly, i.e. he will reach peak fitness too soon, decrease the workload, repetitions and speeds.

- If the horse appears 'sour', i.e. he seems to have lost his interest in jumping and general enthusiasm for his work, rule out any health reasons first. Then it may be necessary to give him a break from training – perhaps turn him out to grass for a couple of weeks or simply ease up on the fittening work to take the pressure off him. Obviously this will affect your programme and the time taken to achieve fitness, but the horse's health is your primary consideration – and if he has gone sour, he won't perform well anyway.

CHAPTER SUMMARY

When training horses we often monitor their fitness almost subconsciously. The experienced trainer knows intuitively whether or not the horses are fit enough for their discipline. However, at the higher levels of competition, when a slight lack of fitness can have disastrous consequences, the need for accurate assessment increases. This is where the heart rate monitor comes in useful.

Whatever means of assessing fitness are used, the most important point to remember is that each horse is an individual. Horses vary in their ability to achieve and maintain fitness and a programme that suits one horse won't automatically suit another. The programme should therefore be modified to suit each individual.